YOUNG READER'S EDITION

THE
HIDING
PLACE

CORRIE TEN BOOM

WITH ELIZABETH & JOHN SHERRILL

ABRIDGED BY LONNIE HULL DUPONT
ILLUSTRATED BY TIM FOLEY

Chosen

a division of Baker Publishing Group
Minneapolis, Minnesota

© 1971 and 1984 by Corrie ten Boom
and Elizabeth and John Sherrill
© 2006, 2015 by Elizabeth and John Sherrill

Published by Chosen Books
11400 Hampshire Avenue South
Bloomington, Minnesota 55438
www.chosenbooks.com

Chosen Books is a division of
Baker Publishing Group, Grand Rapids, Michigan

Printed in the United States of America

The Library of Congress has cataloged a previous edition as follows:

Ten Boom, Corrie.
    The hiding place / Corrie ten Boom with Elizabeth and John Sherrill.
 — 35th anniversary ed.
        p. cm.
    ISBN 0-8007-9405-2 (pbk.)
    1. Ten Boom, Corrie. 2. Ravensbrück (Concentration camp) 3. World
War, 1939–1945—Concentration camps—Germany—Ravensbrück.
    4. World War, 1939–1945—Underground movements—Netherlands.
    5. Netherlands—History—German occupation, 1939–1945. 6. World War,
1939–1945—Personal narratives, Dutch. I. Sherrill, Elizabeth. II. Sherrill,
John L. III. Title.
    D805.5.R38T46   2006
    940.53492092—dc22   2005023916

ISBN 978-0-8007-9627-3

Text abridged by Lonnie Hull DuPont

Material contained in "Since Then" is reprinted with permission from *Guideposts*
magazine. Copyright © 1983 by Guideposts Associates, Inc., Carmel, NY 10512.

Scripture is taken from the King James Version of the Bible. The ten Boom family read the Bible in Dutch, and later, when Corrie and Betsie read it aloud in
Bible studies, they translated it for their audience. The KJV is, therefore, an
approximate translation.

Cover design by Kirk DouPonce, DogEared Design
Interior illustrations by Tim Foley

15 16 17 18 19 20 21   7 6 5 4 3 2 1

CONTENTS

1

THE ONE HUNDREDTH
BIRTHDAY PARTY

I jumped out of bed that morning with one question in my mind—sun or fog? Usually it was fog in January in Holland. I leaned as far as I could from the single window in my bedroom in our building, called the Beje (*bay-yeah*); it was always hard to see the sky from there. Brick walls looked back at me in this crowded center of Haarlem. But I could see a patch of pale sky.

Father's bedroom was directly under mine, but at 77 he slept soundly. *You are not growing younger yourself*, I reminded my reflection in the mirror. I was 45 years old and unmarried. My sister Betsie, seven years older than I and also unmarried, still had that slender grace that made people turn and look after her in the street. Heaven knows it was not her clothes; our little watch shop had never made much money.

Below me down on the street, the doorbell rang. I opened my door and plunged down the steep twisting stairway. Actually, the Beje was two houses. The one in front was a typical old-Haarlem structure, three stories high, two rooms deep, and only one room wide. At some point its  rear wall had been knocked through to join it with the even thinner, steeper house in back of it—which had only three rooms, one on top of the other—and this narrow corkscrew staircase squeezed between the two.

Betsie was at the door ahead of me. An enormous spray of flowers filled the doorway. We searched the bouquet for the card. "Pickwick!" we shouted together.

Pickwick was a wealthy customer who not only bought the very finest watches but often came upstairs to the family part of the house above the shop. His real name was Herman Sluring; Pickwick was the name Betsie and I used between ourselves because he looked like the illustrator's drawing in our copy of Dickens. Herman Sluring was short, bald, and immensely fat, and his eyes were such that you were never quite sure whether he was looking at you or someone else. He was as kind as he was fearsome to look at.

The flowers had come to the side door, the door the family used, opening onto a tiny alleyway, and Betsie and I carried them into the shop. First was the workroom, where watches

8

and clocks were repaired. There was the high bench over which Father had bent for so many years, doing the delicate, painstaking work that was known as the finest in Holland. In the center of the room was my bench, next to mine Hans the apprentice's, and against the wall old Christoffels'.

Beyond the workroom was the customers' part of the shop, with its glass case full of watches. All the wall clocks were striking 7:00 as Betsie and I carried the flowers in. Ever since childhood, I had loved to step into this room where a hundred ticking voices welcomed me. I unlocked the street door and stepped out into the Barteljorisstraat. The other shops up and down the narrow street were still shuttered: the optician's next door, the dress shop, the baker's, Weil's Furriers across the street.

I folded back our shutters and admired the window display. It held a collection of clocks and pocketwatches all at least a hundred years old, all borrowed for the occasion. For today was the shop's one hundredth birthday. In January 1837, Father's father had placed in this window a sign:

Ten Boom
Watches

The doorbell on the alley rang again; more flowers. So it went for an hour, large bouquets and small ones, elaborate pieces and home-grown plants in clay pots. For although the party was for the shop, the affection was for Father. "Haarlem's Grand Old Man" they called him.

When the shop and the workroom would not hold another bouquet, Betsie and I carried them upstairs to the two rooms

above the shop. Though it was twenty years since her death, these were still "Tante Jans' rooms." Tante Jans was Mother's older sister, and her presence lingered in the massive dark furniture she had left behind.

At 7:45 Hans, the apprentice, arrived, and at 8:00 Toos, our saleslady-bookkeeper. Toos was a sour-faced individual whose unpleasant personality had made it impossible for her to keep a job until—ten years ago—she had come to work for Father. Father's gentle courtesy had mellowed her, and though she would never have admitted it, she loved him as fiercely as she disliked the rest of the world. We left Hans and Toos to answer the doorbell and went upstairs to get breakfast.

I set out three plates. The dining room was in the house at the rear, five steps higher than the shop but lower than Tante Jans' rooms. This room with its single window looking into the alley was the heart of the home. We used only a corner of the table now, Father, Betsie, and I, but to me the rest of the family was still there. There was Mama's chair, and the three aunts' chairs (not only Tante Jans but Mama's other two sisters had also lived with us). Next to me had sat my other sister, Nollie, and Willem, the only boy.

Nollie and Willem had homes of their own now, and Mama and the aunts were dead, but still I seemed to see them here. Their chairs had not stayed empty long. Father could never bear a house without children, and whenever he heard of a child in need of a home a new face appeared at the table. Out of his watch shop that never made much money, he fed and cared for eleven more children after his own four were grown. Now these, too, had grown up and married or gone off to work, and so I laid three plates on the table.

Betsie brought the coffee in from the tiny kitchen off the dining room, and we heard Father's step coming down the staircase. He went slowly now on the stairs; but still as punctual as one of his own watches, he entered the dining room, as he had every morning since I could remember, at 8:10.

Father's hair and beard were now as white as the tablecloth. But his blue eyes behind the thick round spectacles were as mild and merry as ever. He gazed from one of us to the other.

"Corrie, dear! My dear Betsie! How lovely you both look!"

He bowed his head and said the blessing.

How could we have guessed as we sat there—two middle-aged sisters and an old man—that we were about to be given adventures such as we had never dreamed of? Adventure and anguish, horror and heaven were just around the corner. In that room on that day, we did not know.

Father took the big Bible from its shelf as Toos and Hans came in. Scripture reading at 8:30 each morning for all who were in the house was another of the points around which life in the Beje revolved. Father turned to the gospel of Luke, where we had left off yesterday. He looked up.

"Where is Christoffels?"

Christoffels was the third and only other employee in the shop, a little man who looked older than Father, though actually he was ten years younger. I remembered the day years earlier when he first came into the shop, so ragged that I had assumed he was a street beggar. I was about to send him up to the kitchen, where Betsie kept a pot of soup simmering, when he announced with great dignity that he was considering permanent employment and was offering his services first to us.

We learned Christoffels belonged to an almost vanished trade, the clockmender who trudged on foot throughout the land, regulating and repairing the tall pendulum clocks that were the pride of every Dutch farmhouse. Father hired him on the spot. "They're the finest clockmen anywhere," he told me later, "these wandering clocksmiths. There's not a repair job they haven't handled with just the tools in their sack."

People all over Haarlem brought their clocks to Christoffels. What he did with his wages we never knew; he had remained as threadbare as ever, though Christoffels' most notable quality was his pride.

Now, for the first time ever, Christoffels was late.

Father polished his glasses with his napkin and started to read, his deep voice lingering over the words. Eventually we heard Christoffels' shuffling steps on the stairs. The door opened and all of us gasped. Christoffels was resplendent in a new black suit, checkered vest, white shirt, tie and stiff starched collar.

"Christoffels, my dear associate," Father murmured in his formal way, "what joy to see you." And he resumed his Bible reading.

Soon the doorbells were ringing, both the shop bell on the street and the bell in the alley. Toos and I hurried to the doors. Before long a steady stream of guests climbed the narrow staircase to Tante Jans' rooms, where Father sat almost lost in a thicket of flowers. As I helped one of the older guests up the steep stairs, Betsie seized my arm.

"We need Nollie's cups right away!"

"I'll go get them!"

Our sister, Nollie, and her husband were coming as soon as their six children got home from school. I dashed down the stairs, took my coat and my bicycle from inside the alley door, and set out over the bumpy brick streets. Nollie and her husband lived about a mile and a half from the Beje, outside the center of the city. I pedaled there often.

How could I foresee, as I zipped around corners, that one day I would stand on Nollie's street with my heart thudding in my throat, daring to go no closer to her house for fear of what was taking place there?

Today I careened onto the sidewalk and burst through the door with never a knock. "Nollie, we need the cups right now!"

Nollie came out of the kitchen, her pretty face flushed with baking. "They're all packed by the door. I wish I could go with you—but I've got more still to bake."

"You're *all* coming, aren't you?"

"Yes, Corrie, Peter will be there."

I loved all my nieces and nephews. But Peter . . . well, was Peter. At thirteen he was a musical prodigy and a rascal and the pride of my life.

The Beje was even more crowded when I got back. The mayor of Haarlem was there. And the postman and the trolley motorman and half a dozen policemen from the Haarlem Police Headquarters just around the corner.

After lunch the children started coming, and as children always did, they went straight to Father. The older ones sat on the floor around him; the smallest ones climbed into his lap. In addition to his twinkling eyes, Father ticked. Watches lying on a shelf run differently from watches carried about, so Father always wore the ones he was regulating. His suit jackets had inside pockets fitted with hooks for a dozen watches, so wherever he went the hum of hundreds of little wheels went with him. Now with a child on each knee and ten more crowded close, he drew from another pocket his heavy cross-shaped winding key, each of the four ends shaped for a different size clock. With a flick of his finger, he made it spin, gleaming, glinting. . . .

A shriek below told me that Pickwick had arrived. We sometimes forgot, we who loved him, what a shock the first sight of him could be to a stranger. I hurried down to the door and got him upstairs. He sank his bulk into a chair beside Father, fixed one eye on me, the other on the ceiling, and said, "Five lumps, please."

Pickwick loved children as much as Father did, but while children took to Father on sight, Pickwick had to win them. He had one trick that never failed. I brought him his cup of coffee, thick with sugar, and watched him look around in mock consternation. "But, my dear Cornelia!" he cried, "there's no table to set it on!" He glanced out of one wide-set eye to make sure the children were watching. "Well, it's a lucky thing I brought my own!" With that he set cup and saucer on his own protruding paunch. I never knew a child who could resist it; soon a respectful circle had gathered round him.

Now Nollie and her family arrived. "Tante Corrie!" Peter greeted me innocently. "You don't *look* one hundred years old!" Before I could swat him, he was sitting at Tante Jans' upright piano, filling the house with melody. People called out requests, and soon the whole room was singing.

The workroom and shop were even more crowded with well-wishers than the upstairs rooms, as all through the afternoon they kept coming, the people who counted themselves Father's friends. Young and old, poor and rich, scholarly gentlemen and illiterate servant girls—only to Father did it seem that they were all alike. That was Father's secret: not that he overlooked the differences in people, but that he did not know they were there.

I said good-bye to some guests at the door and stood for a moment gazing up and down the Barteljorisstraat, wondering what was keeping Willem and his family. I still had a great deal of little-sister worship for this big brother, five years older than I, a minister and the only Ten Boom who had ever been to college. Willem saw things. He knew what was going on in the world.

Much that he saw was frightening. Ten years ago, he had written in his doctoral thesis, done in Germany, that a terrible evil was taking root in that land. Right at the university, he said, seeds were being planted of a contempt for human life such as the world had never seen. Those who read his paper had laughed.

Now people were not laughing about Germany. Most of the good clocks came from there, and recently firms with whom we had dealt for years were simply and mysteriously "out of business." Willem believed it was part of a deliberate and large-scale move against Jews; every one of the closed businesses was Jewish.

In Hilversum, Willem scrimped and saved enough money to build a home for elderly Jews and the elderly of all faiths. But in the last few months, the home had been deluged with younger arrivals—all Jews and all from Germany. These frightened people brought with them tales of a mounting madness.

I picked up a fresh pot of coffee in the kitchen and continued with it upstairs to Tante Jans' rooms. As I set down the pot, I asked a group of men, "This man in Germany, does he want war?"

I knew it was poor talk for a party. A chill of silence fell over the table.

At that moment Willem entered the room. Behind him came Tine, his wife, and their four children. But every eye in the room settled on the figure whose arm Willem held. The man was a Jew in his thirties in a broad-brimmed black hat and long black coat. His face had been burned. In front of his right ear dangled a gray and frazzled ringlet. The rest of his beard was gone, leaving only a raw wound.

"This is Herr Gutlieber," Willem announced in German. "He just arrived in Hilversum this morning. Herr Gutlieber, my father." Willem continued rapidly in Dutch. "Teenaged boys in Munich set fire to his beard."

Father rose from his chair and eagerly shook the newcomer's hand. I brought him a cup of coffee and a plate of cookies. How grateful I was now for Father's insistence that his children speak German and English almost as soon as Dutch.

Herr Gutlieber sat down stiffly on the edge of a chair and fixed his eyes on the cup in his lap. I pulled up a chair beside him and talked about the weather, and around us conversation began again.

And so the shadow fell across us that afternoon in 1937, but it rested lightly. Nobody dreamed that this tiny cloud would grow and that in this darkness each of us would be called to play a role: Father and Betsie and Willem—even the funny old Beje.

That evening, I climbed the stairs to my room. Childhood scenes rushed at me, strangely close and urgent. Today I know that such memories are the key not to the past, but to the future. I know that the experiences of our lives, when we let God use them, become the mysterious preparation for the work He will give us to do. But I did not know that then.

2

FULL TABLE

I was six years old. Betsie stood me in front of the mirror and helped me dress for my first day of school.

Eight-year-old Nollie and I shared the bedroom at the top of the Beje. She and I were almost the same age and played together, but Betsie, at thirteen, seemed almost an adult to me. She had always seemed older because she could not run and roughhouse the way other children did. Betsie had been born with pernicious anemia. While the rest of us played tag or had skate races down frozen canals in winter, she did dull things like embroidery.

There were many living at the Beje. Tante Jans, Mama's older sister, had moved in with us to spend, as she put it, "what few days remain to me," though she was not very old. The house was already crowded by the earlier arrivals of Mama's other two sisters, Tante Bep and Tante Anna.

Tante Jans took the two second-story rooms of the front house. In the first room she wrote the Christian tracts for which she was known all over Holland, and in the second received the well-to-do ladies who supported this work. For sleep she partitioned off a cubicle just large enough to hold a bed.

Above Tante Jans' two rooms were four small rooms. The first one was Tante Bep's. Behind it, strung like railroad compartments off a narrow aisle, were Tante Anna's, Betsie's, and our brother Willem's. Five steps up from these rooms, in the second house behind, was Nollie's and my small room. Beneath us was Mama and Father's room, and beneath theirs the dining room with the kitchen off to the side.

As I descended the steep stairs that morning when I was six, on my first day of school, I had an awful feeling. How was I to leave this house above the watch shop, leave Mama and Father and the aunts, leave behind everything that was certain and well-loved? The school was only a block and a half away, and Nollie had gone there two years without difficulty. But Nollie was different from me; she was pretty and well-behaved.

As I rounded the final curve of the stairway, the solution came to me, so clear and simple that I laughed out loud. I just would not go to school! I would stay here and help Tante Anna with the cooking, Mama would teach me to read, and I would never go into that strange building at all. Relief flooded me.

Tante Bep, with her disapproving scowl, was the oldest of the aunts and the one we children liked least. For thirty years she had worked as a governess in wealthy families, and she continually compared our behavior with that of the youngsters she was used to.

It was 8:12. Breakfast had already begun.

"Two minutes late!" cried Willem triumphantly.

"The Waller children were never late," said Tante Bep.

"But they're here!" said Father. "And the room is brighter!"

We sisters took our seats. I looked around the table trying to decide which adult would be most enthusiastic about my decision to stay at home. Father put a high importance on education. He had had to stop school to go to work in the watch shop, and though he had taught himself history, theology and literature in five languages, he always regretted the missed schooling. He would want me to go—and whatever Father wanted, Mama wanted.

Tante Anna? She had often told me she could not manage without me to run errands up and down the steep stairs. Since Mama was not strong, Tante Anna did the housework for our family of nine. She was the youngest of the four sisters, with a spirit as generous as Mama's. Yes, she would be my ally.

A deep dramatic intake of breath made us all look up. Tante Jans was standing in the kitchen doorway, a glass of liquid in her hand. She closed her eyes, lifted the glass to her lips, and drained it down. Then with a sigh she sat down.

"And yet," she said, as though we had been discussing the subject, "what do doctors know? What good does anything do when one's day arrives?"

I glanced round the table; no one was smiling. Tante Jans' preoccupation with death might have been funny, but it wasn't. Young as I was, I knew that fear is never funny.

"And yet, Jans," Father remonstrated gently, "medicine has prolonged many a life."

Fortunately the shop people arrived and Father took down the Bible from its shelf. He put on his rimless spectacles and began to read: "Thy word is a lamp unto my feet, and a light unto my path. . . . Thou art my hiding place and my shield: I hope in thy word."

What kind of hiding place? I wondered idly. What was there to hide from?

When at last Father closed the big volume, Nollie, Willem, and Betsie were on their feet. Next minute they raced down the stairs and out the alley door. The shopworkers left for work. Only then did the five adults notice me still seated at the table.

"Corrie!" cried Mama. "Have you forgotten you're a big girl now? Today you go to school too!"

"I'm not going."

There was a startled silence, broken by everybody at once.

"When I was a girl—" Tante Jans began.

"Mrs. Waller's children—" from Tante Bep.

But Father's deep voice drowned them out. "Of course she's not going alone! Nollie forgot to wait, that's all. Corrie is going with me."

He wrapped my hand in his and led me from the room. There was a railing along the bottom five steps. I grabbed it with my free hand and held on. Skilled watchmaker's fingers closed over mine and gently unwound them. Howling and struggling, I was led away from the world I knew into a bigger, stranger one. . . .

Mondays, Father took the train to Amsterdam to get the correct time from the Naval Observatory, and I would go with him. The train trip to Amsterdam was a wonderful ride. The close-wedged buildings of Haarlem gave way to the flat Dutch farmland stretching to the horizon, ruler-straight canals sweeping past the window. Then came Amsterdam, with its strange streets and canals.

Father always arrived a couple of hours early in order to visit the wholesalers who supplied him with watches and parts. Many of these were Jews, and these were the visits we both liked best. After a brief discussion of business, Father would draw a small Bible from his traveling case; the wholesaler, whose beard would be even longer than Father's, would snatch a book or a scroll out of a drawer, and clap a prayer cap

onto his head. And then the two of them would be off, arguing, comparing, interrupting, contradicting—reveling in each other's company.

Just when I decided that this time I had been forgotten, the wholesaler would catch sight of me and strike his forehead with the heel of his hand.

"A guest in my gates and I have offered her no refreshment!" Springing up, he would rummage into cupboards, and before long I would be holding on my lap a plate of the most delicious treats in the world—honey cakes and date cakes and a kind of confection of nuts, fruits, and sugar.

By five minutes before noon we were back at the train station, standing at a point on the platform with a good view of the tower of the Naval Observatory. On the top of the tower where it could be seen by ships in the harbor was a tall shaft with two movable arms. At the stroke of 12:00 noon each day the arms dropped. Father would stand at his vantage point on the platform, holding his pocket watch. There! Now he could carry home the correct time, accurate to the second.

On the train trip home we talked—about different things as the years passed. Betsie's graduation from school in spite of the months missed with illness. Whether Willem would get the scholarship that would let him go on to the university. Betsie starting work as Father's bookkeeper in the shop. Sometimes I would bring up things that were troubling me. I treasured those times with Father.

I followed Mama and Nollie up a dark flight of stairs where cobwebs clutched at our hair. We were going to see one of the poor families in the neighborhood whom Mama had adopted.

Mama was always cooking up nourishing soups for forgotten old men and pale young mothers—on days, that is, when she herself was strong enough to stand at the stove.

The night before, a baby had died, and with a basket of fresh bread Mama was making a call on the family. She toiled up the stairs, stopping often for breath. At the top a door opened. Mama went at once to the young mother, but I stood frozen on the threshold. To the right of the door, still in the crib, was the baby.

I stared at the tiny unmoving form with my heart thudding strangely against my ribs. For a while curiosity and terror struggled in me. At last I put one finger on the small hand. It was cold.

For all Tante Jans' talk about it, death had been only a word. Now I knew that it could really happen—if to the baby, then to Mama, to Father, to Betsie!

That night, still shivering with that cold, I followed Nollie to our room and crept into bed beside her. At last we heard Father's footsteps. It was the best moment, when he came up to tuck us in. We never fell asleep until he had arranged the blankets in his special way and laid his hand for a moment on each head.

That night as he stepped through the door, I burst into tears. "You can't die!" I sobbed. "You can't!"

"We went to see Mrs. Hoog," Nollie explained.

Father sat down on the edge of the narrow bed. "Corrie," he began gently, "when you and I go to Amsterdam—when do I give you your ticket?"

I considered this. "Just before we get on the train."

"Exactly. And our wise Father in heaven knows when we're going to need things, too. Don't run ahead of Him, Corrie. When the time comes that some of us will have to die, you will look into your heart and find the strength you need—just in time."

3

KAREL

I met Karel at a party at the Beje. Willem introduced him and he shook hands with us one by one. I took that long strong hand, looked up into those deep brown eyes, and fell in love.

Karel seemed unaware of me. I was only fourteen, while he and Willem were already university men. It was enough, I felt, to be in the same room with Karel.

I thought I was going to love him forever.

Two years later I saw Karel again when Nollie and I visited Willem at the university. Willem's room was in a private home. He gathered both Nollie and me into a bear hug. A second later the door slammed open and in burst four of his friends—tall, deep-voiced young men. Among them was Karel.

Willem introduced Nollie and me around. When he came to Karel, Karel interrupted. "We know each other already."

He bowed slightly. "Do you remember? We met at a party at your home." I glanced from Karel to Nollie—but no, he was looking straight at me.

Soon the young men were seated at our feet on the floor, all talking at once. Nollie joined in. She was eighteen and had started college to become a teacher, so she chattered easily and knowledgeably about things of interest to students.

"And you, Corrie. Will you become a teacher, too?"

Karel was smiling at me. I felt myself blush.

"No. I'll stay home with Mama and Tante Anna."

It came out so short and flat. Why did I say so little when I wanted to say so much?

That spring I finished school and took over the work of the household. It had always been planned that I would do this, but now there was an added reason. Tante Bep had tuberculosis. Around the clock Tante Anna nursed her sister, many nights getting no sleep at all, and so the cooking and washing and cleaning for the family fell to me. I loved the work, and except for Tante Bep would have been completely happy. Over Tante Bep lay the shadow not only of her illness but of her whole disappointed life.

I spoke about it once to Mama. She too was more and more often in bed. But when Mama was not supplying the neighborhood with baby clothes from her flying knitting needles, she was composing cheery messages for shut-ins all over Haarlem. The fact that she herself had been shut in much of her life never seemed to occur to her.

"Mama," I said as I sat down beside her, "can't we do something for Tante Bep? She is so unhappy here."

Mama laid down her pen. "Corrie," she said, "Bep is as happy here with us—no more and no less—than she was anywhere else."

I did not understand.

"Do you know when she started praising the Wallers?" Mama went on. "The day she left them. While she was there, she had nothing but complaints. The Wallers couldn't compare with the van Hooks, where she'd been before. But at the van Hooks' she'd been miserable. Happiness isn't something that depends on our surroundings, Corrie. It's something we make inside ourselves."

When Tante Bep died, Mama and Tante Anna redoubled their cooking and sewing for the needy, as though realizing how brief was anyone's lifetime. As for Tante Jans, she exclaimed at odd moments, "My own sister. Why, it might as well have been me!"

A year or so after Tante Bep's death, a new doctor took over house calls. His name was Jan van Veen, and with him came his young sister and nurse, Tine van Veen. It was Dr. van Veen who discovered that Tante Jans had diabetes.

In those days this was a death sentence as surely as tuberculosis had been. Tante Jans went straight to bed on hearing the news. But inaction went poorly with her personality. One morning to everyone's surprise, she appeared for breakfast precisely at 8:10, with the announcement that doctors were often wrong. "All these tests and tubes," said Tante Jans, "what do they really prove?"

From then on she threw herself into writing, speaking, and launching projects. Only those of us who knew her best were aware, beneath all the activity, of the fear that drove her.

Her disease meant that each week a test had to be made to determine the sugar content of her blood, and this was a complicated process requiring either Dr. van Veen or his sister to come to the house. Eventually Tine van Veen taught me to run the weekly test myself each Friday. There were several steps involved. If the mixture remained clear when heated, all was well. If ever it turned black, I was to notify Dr. van Veen.

That spring Willem came home for a holiday. He had graduated from the university and was now in his last months of theological school. One evening during his visit we were all sitting around the dining room table. Father had thirty watches spread out before him; he marked in a little notebook: "two seconds lost," "five seconds gained," while Willem read aloud.

The bell in the alley rang. Outside the dining room window a mirror faced the alley door so that we could see who was there before going down to open it. I glanced into it and sprang up from the table. For at the door, a bouquet of daffodils in her hands, was Tine van Veen. Whether it was the soft spring night that put it in my mind, or Willem's dramatic, pulpit-trained voice, I suddenly knew that these two people must meet.

"For your mother, Corrie," Tine said, holding out the flowers as I opened the door.

"No, no, you carry the flowers! You look beautiful with them!" And I pushed the startled girl up the stairs.

I prodded her through the dining room door, straining to see Willem's reaction. I knew exactly how it would be. My life was lived just then in romantic novels, and I had played this scene where hero meets heroine a thousand times.

Willem rose slowly to his feet, his eyes never leaving Tine's. Father stood up too. "Miss van Veen," Father said, "allow me to present to you our son, Willem. Willem, this is the young lady of whose kindness you have heard us speak."

I doubt either one heard the introduction. They were staring at each other as though there were not another soul in the room.

Willem and Tine were married two months after his ordination. During all the weeks of getting ready, one thought stood out in my mind: *Karel will be there.* The wedding day dawned cool and sparkling. My eyes picked Karel from the crowd in front of the church, dressed in top hat and tails as were all the male guests, but incomparably the handsomest there.

As for me, I felt that a transformation had taken place since he had seen me last. The difference between my 21 years and his 26 was not as big as it had once been. But more than that, I earnestly believed—and all the books agreed—that I would look beautiful to the man who loved me.

"Corrie?"

In front of me stood Karel, tall black hat in his hands, his eyes searching my face.

"Yes, it's me!" I said, laughing up at him.

"But you're so grown up. I've always thought of you as the little girl with the enormous blue eyes." He stared at me a little longer and then added softly, "Now the little girl is a lady, and a lovely one." Suddenly the organ music swelling from the open door was for us, the arm he offered me was the moon, and my gloved hand resting upon it the only thing that kept me from soaring right over the peaked rooftops of Haarlem.

It was a rainy Friday morning when my eyes told me what at first my brain refused to grasp. The liquid in the glass beaker on the kitchen stove was black.

I leaned against the sink and shut my eyes. I went over in my mind the different steps, looked at the vials of chemicals, the measuring spoons. All just the same as I had always done.

The liquid was black.

Clutching the beaker,

I pounded down the steps.

I burst into the shop with the telltale beaker.

"Betsie!" I cried. "It's black!"

Betsie put her arms around me. Behind me, Father came into the shop. His eyes traveled from the beaker to Betsie to me.

"You did it exactly right, Corrie?"

"I'm afraid so, Father."

"I am sure you did, my dear. But we must have the doctor's verdict."

I poured the liquid into a small bottle and ran to Dr. van Veen's, where he took the bottle into his small laboratory.

"There is no mistake, Corrie," he said. "Your aunt has three weeks at the very most."

We held a family conference in the watch shop when I got back. We agreed that Tante Jans must know at once. "We will tell her together," Father decided, "though I will speak the necessary words."

Our little procession filed up the steps to Tante Jans' rooms. She was sitting at her table, working on a project. As she saw the number of people entering the room, she laid down her pen. She looked from one face to another, until she came to mine and gave a little gasp of comprehension. This was Friday, and I had not yet come up with the results of the test.

"My dear sister-in-law," Father began gently, "there is a joyous journey which each of God's children sooner or later sets out on. And, Jans, some must go to their Father empty-handed, but you will run to Him with hands full!"

"All your projects . . ." Tante Anna ventured.

"Your writings . . ." Mama added.

"The funds you've raised . . ." said Betsie.

"Your talks . . ." I began.

But our well-meant words were useless. Tante Jans put her hands over her eyes and began to cry. "Empty!" she choked at last. "How can we bring anything to God? What does He care for our little tricks and trinkets?"

As we listened in disbelief, she lowered her hands and, with tears coursing down her face, whispered, "Dear Jesus, I thank You that we must come with empty hands. I thank You that You have done all—all—on the cross, and that all we need in life or death is to be sure of this."

Mama threw her arms around her and they clung together. But I stood rooted to the spot, knowing that I had seen a mystery.

It was Father's train ticket, given at the moment itself.

Four months after Tante Jans' funeral the invitation came to Willem's first sermon. In the Dutch Reformed Church, a minister's first sermon in his first church was the most solemn and joyous occasion. Family and friends would come from great distances and stay for days.

From his own assistant pastorate, Karel wrote that he would be there and looked forward to seeing us all again. I endowed that word "all" with special meaning and packed in a delirium of anticipation.

Three days after we got there, I answered Willem and Tine's front door, and there stood Karel, dusty from the train trip. He tossed his bag past me into the hall, seized my hand, and drew me out into the June sunshine. "It's a lovely day, Corrie!" he cried. "Come walking!"

From then on, Karel and I would go walking each day. We wandered down the country lanes that wound in every direction away from the village. One sunlit day followed another. Our walks lasted longer.

Often we talked about Karel's future, and suddenly we were speaking not about what Karel was going to do, but about what *we* were going to do. We imagined that we had a house to decorate and rejoiced to discover that we had the same ideas about furniture, flowers, even the same favorite colors. Only about children did we disagree: Karel wanted four, while I held out for six.

All this while the word *marriage* was never spoken.

One day when Karel was out, Willem came to me with two cups of coffee in his hands. Tine with a cup of her own was just behind him.

"Corrie," Willem said, handing me the coffee and speaking as though with effort, "has Karel led you to believe that he is—"

"Serious?" Tine finished his sentence.

A blush set my cheeks burning. "Why?"

Willem's face reddened, too. "Because, Corrie, this is something that can never be. You don't know Karel's family. They've wanted one thing since he was a small child. They've built their whole lives around it. Karel is to . . . 'marry well' is the way they put it."

"But what about what Karel wants? He's not a child now!"

Willem fixed his eyes on mine. "He will do it, Corrie. I don't say he wants it. To him it's just a fact of life like any other. At the university, when we'd talk about girls we liked, he'd always say at the end, 'Of course, I could never marry her. It would kill my mother.'"

The hot coffee scalded my mouth. I made my escape to the garden where there was hardly a flower that Karel and I had not looked at together, that did not have a bit of our feeling for each other still clinging to it. Willem might know more than I did about many things—but not when it came to romance! Things like money, social prestige, family expectations, why, in the books they vanished like rain clouds.

Karel left a week or so later, and his last words made my heart soar. Only months afterward did I remember how strangely he spoke them. We said good-bye outdoors, and if part of me was disappointed that he still had not proposed, another part of me was content just to be beside him. Suddenly he seized my hands.

"Corrie, write to me!" he said pleadingly. "Write me about the Beje! I want to know everything. I want every detail of that beautiful, crumbling old house! Oh, Corrie, it's the happiest home in Holland!"

And so it was, indeed, when the others and I returned to the Beje. It had always been a happy place, but now each event seemed to glow because I could share it with Karel. Every meal I cooked was an offering to him, each shining pot a poem, every sweep of the broom an act of love.

His letters did not come as often as mine went singing to him, but I put this down to his work. The minister he was assisting, he wrote, had turned the parish calling over to him, and church members expected frequent visits from the clergy. As time went by, his letters came more seldom. I made up for it with mine and went humming my way though the summer and fall.

One nippy November day, the doorbell rang. I flung open the alley door and there was Karel.

Beside him was a young woman.

She smiled at me. I took in the hat with its sweeping feather, the fur collar, the white-gloved hand resting on his arm. Karel was saying, "Corrie, I want you to meet my fiancée."

I must have said something. I only recall how my family came to the rescue, shaking hands, taking coats, finding chairs, so that I would not have to do or say anything for the next half hour.

Finally it passed. I managed to shake her hand, then Karel's hand, and to wish them happiness. Betsie took them to the door. Before it clicked shut, I was fleeing up the stairs to my own room at the top of the house.

How long I lay on my bed sobbing for the one love of my life I do not know. Later, I heard Father's footsteps coming up the stairs. For a moment I was a little girl again, waiting for him to tuck the blankets tight. But suddenly I was afraid Father might say, "There'll be someone else soon." For in some deep part of me I knew already that there would never be anyone else.

Of course he did not say the false, idle words.

"Corrie," he began instead, "do you know what hurts so very much? It's love. Love is the strongest force in the world, and when it is blocked that means pain. There are two things we can do when this happens. We can kill the love so that it stops hurting. Then of course part of us dies, too. Or we can ask God to open up another route for that love to travel.

"God loves Karel—even more than you do—and if you ask Him, He will give you His love for this man, a love nothing can prevent, nothing destroy. Whenever we cannot love in the human way, Corrie, God can give us the perfect way."

I did not know, as I listened to Father's footsteps winding back down the stairs, that he had given me more than the key to this hard moment. I did not know that he had put into my hands

36

the secret that would open far darker rooms than this—places where there was not, on a human level, anything to love at all.

But just then, my task was to give up my feeling for Karel without giving up the joy and wonder that had grown with it. So lying there on my bed, I whispered the enormous prayer:

"Lord, I give to You the way I feel about Karel, my thoughts about our future—oh, You know! Everything! Give me Your way of seeing Karel instead. Help me to love him that way."

Even as I said the words I fell asleep.

4

THE WATCH SHOP

Not long after the visit from Karel, Mama had a stroke. For two months she lay unconscious in bed while we took turns at her side. And then one morning, her eyes opened and she looked around her. Eventually she regained the use of her arms and legs enough to be able to move about with assistance, though her hands would never again hold her knitting needles.

We moved her to Tante Jans' front room, where she could watch the busy life of the Barteljorisstraat. Her mind was as active as ever, but the power of speech did not return—with the exception of three words: *yes*, *no*, and *Corrie*. Now Mama called everybody "Corrie."

It was astonishing, though, the quality of life she was able to lead in that crippled body. Watching her during the three years of her paralysis, I made another discovery about love.

Mama's love had always been the kind that acted itself out with soup pot and sewing basket. Now that these things were taken away, she sat in her chair at the window and loved us. She loved the people she saw in the street—and beyond. I learned that love is larger than the walls that shut it in.

Nollie's conversation at the dinner table was more and more about a young fellow teacher at the school where she taught, Flip van Woerden. Eventually the young man called on Father to ask for Nollie's hand in marriage, and there was a Ten Boom wedding.

Nollie was radiant that day in her long white dress. But it was Mama I could not take my eyes off. She seemed young and girlish, eyes sparkling with joy at this great occasion. Betsie and I took her into the church early, and I believe that most of the van Woerden family and friends never dreamed the gracious and smiling lady in the first pew could neither walk alone nor speak.

Not until Nollie and Flip came down the aisle together did I think for the first time of my own dreams of such a moment with Karel. I glanced at Betsie, so tall and lovely. Betsie had always known that, because of her health, she could not have children, and for that reason had decided never to marry. Now I was 27, Betsie in her mid-30s, and I knew that this was the way it was going to be: Betsie and I, the unmarried daughters living at home in the Beje.

It was a happy thought, not a sad one. I knew for certain that God had answered my prayer four years ago, because with the thought of Karel came not the slightest trace of hurt. "Bless Karel, Lord Jesus," I murmured under my breath. "And bless her. Keep them close to one another and to You." I knew that was a prayer that could not have sprung unaided from Corrie ten Boom.

But the great miracle of the day came later. To close the service we had chosen Mama's favorite hymn, "Fairest Lord Jesus." As I stood singing it, I heard, behind me in the pew, Mama singing, too. Mama, who could not speak four words, sang the beautiful lines without a stammer, all the way through. It was a gift to us from God.

In spite of that moment, her speech never improved, and four weeks later, in her sleep, Mama slipped away from us forever.

In November that year Betsie began to sniff and sneeze. Father decided she must not sit behind the cashier's table, where the shop door let in the winter air. But Christmas was coming, the shop's busiest time.

Tante Anna insisted she could cook and look after Betsie. So I settled in behind Betsie's table, writing down sales and repair charges, recording cash spent for parts and supplies, and leafing through records in growing disbelief. There was no system here anywhere! No way to tell whether a bill had been paid, no way in fact to tell if we were making money or losing it.

Of course Father was as innocent of business know-how as his father had been before him. He would work for days on a difficult repair problem and then forget to send a bill. The more rare the watch, the less he was able to think of

40

money. "A man should pay for the privilege of working on such a watch!" he would say.

One day I bought a new set of ledgers. Many nights after the door was locked, I sat for hours poring over inventories and statements. I developed a system of billing, and more and more, my columns of figures began to correspond to actual transactions.

I discovered that I loved it. I had always felt happy in this little shop with its tiny voices and shelves of small shining faces. But now I discovered that I liked the business side of it, too, the world of trade.

I knew that Betsie's cold had settled in her chest and threatened to turn into pneumonia, as her colds always did. I would reproach myself for being anything but distressed at the present arrangement. At night when I would hear her racking cough, I would pray with all my heart for her to be better at once.

Then one evening two days before Christmas, when I had closed up the shop for the night, Betsie came bursting in from the alley with her arms full of flowers. Her eyes when she saw me were like a guilty child's.

"For Christmas, Corrie!" she pleaded. "We have to have flowers for Christmas!"

"Betsie!" I exploded. "No wonder you're not getting better!"

"I've stayed in bed most of the time, honestly—" she stopped while great coughs shook her. "I've only got up for really important things."

I put her to bed and then prowled the rooms with newly opened eyes, looking for Betsie's "important things." Betsie had made beautiful changes everywhere. Things that would never have occurred to me, things that make a home.

It became obvious that we had divided the work backward. Once we swapped responsibilties, it was astonishing how well everything went. The house had been clean under my care; under Betsie's it glowed. The food budget, which had barely survived my visits to the butcher and the baker, stretched under Betsie's management to include all kinds of delicious things.

The soup kettle and the coffeepot on the back of the stove, which I never seemed to find time for, were simmering again the first week Betsie took over, and soon a stream of postmen and police, wobbly old men, and shivering errand boys were pausing inside our alley door to cup their hands around hot mugs, just as they had done when Mama was in charge.

Meanwhile, I found joy in my work I had never dreamed of. I realized I wanted to do even more—I wanted to learn watch repair itself. Father eagerly took on the job of teaching me. I quickly learned the parts, the tools, and the techniques, and I became the first licensed woman watchmaker in Holland.

So was established the pattern our lives were to follow for over twenty years. When Father had put the Bible away after breakfast, he and I went downstairs to the shop while Betsie plotted magic with three potatoes and a pound of meat. With my eyes on income-and-outlay, the shop did better. We were able to hire a saleslady for the front room while Father and I worked in back.

There was a constant procession through this little back room. Sometimes it was a customer; most often it was simply a visitor—from a laborer with wooden *klompen* on his feet to a business owner—all bringing their problems to Father. Often he would bow his head and pray for the answer.

He prayed over the work, too. There were not many repair problems he had not encountered. But occasionally one

would come along that baffled even him. I would hear him say: "Lord, You turn the wheels of the galaxies. You know what makes the planets spin, and You know what makes this watch run. . . ." The answers to these prayers seemed often to come in the night. Many mornings I would find the watch that we had left in a hundred pieces fitted together and ticking merrily.

Even before Tante Anna's death, the empty beds in the Beje were filled with the succession of foster children who for over ten years kept the old walls ringing with laughter. Willem and Nollie were having families—Willem and Tine four children, Nollie and Flip six. Willem had started his nursing home in Hilversum, thirty miles from Haarlem.

Nollie's family we saw more often, as their school—of which Flip was now principal—was in Haarlem. Most days one or another of their six was at the Beje to visit Opa at his workbench or peer into Tante Betsie's mixing bowl or race up and down the winding steps with the foster children.

We first discovered young Peter's musical gift around our radio—a large table model with an ornate shell-shaped speaker that brought us many years of joy. One Sunday afternoon when Nollie and her family were listening to a concert with us, Peter spoke up in the middle of a Brahms concerto.

"It's funny they put a bad piano on the radio."

"What do you mean, Peter?" asked Father.

"One of the notes is wrong."

The rest of us exchanged glances: What could an eight-year-old know? But Father led the boy to Tante Jans' old upright. "Which note, Peter?"

Peter struck the keys up the scale till he reached B above middle C. "This one," he said.

Then everyone in the room heard it: The B on the concert piano was flat.

I spent the rest of the afternoon beside Peter on the piano bench, uncovering a phenomenal musical talent. Peter became my music student until—in about six months—he had learned everything I knew and went on to more expert teachers.

Life for Father, Betsie, and me stayed essentially the same. Our foster children grew up and went away to jobs or to marry. The hundredth anniversary came and went; the following day Father and I were back at our workbenches as always.

Even the people we passed on our daily walks were perfectly predictable. I went with Father on his daily stroll through the downtown streets. We took our walk always at the same time, after the midday dinner and before the shop reopened at two, and always over the same route. Since other Haarlemers were just as regular in their habits, we knew exactly whom we would meet. Many of those we nodded to were old friends or customers, others we knew only from this daily encounter. Father tipped his hat to all.

While Haarlem and the rest of Holland strolled and bowed and swept its steps, the neighbors on our east geared for war. We knew what was happening. Often on the radio we would pick up a voice from Germany—a voice that only screamed. Even-tempered Betsie reacted most strongly, hurtling from her chair to shut off the radio.

But when letters to Jewish suppliers in Germany came back marked "Address Unknown," we still believed that it was primarily a German problem. "How long are they going to stand for it?" we said. "They won't put up with that man for long."

Once, the changes in Germany reached inside our little shop. Germans frequently came to work under Father for a while, for his reputation reached beyond Holland. So when a good-looking young man appeared with apprentice papers from a good firm in Berlin, Father hired him without hesitation. Otto told us proudly that he belonged to the Hitler Youth. "The world will see what Germans can do," he said often.

Otto's first morning at work he came upstairs for coffee and Bible reading with the other employees; after that he sat alone down in the shop. When we asked him why, he said that Father was reading from the Old Testament, which, he informed us, was the Jews' "Book of Lies."

I was shocked, but Father was only sorrowful. "He has been taught wrong," he told me. "By watching us, seeing that we love this Book and are truthful people, he will realize his error."

In the end, Father fired Otto—the first employee he had ever discharged in more than sixty years in business. It was Otto's treatment of the old clockmender Christoffels that brought it about.

From the very first I had been baffled by his brusqueness with the old man. It was not what he did, but what he did not do. No standing back to let the older man go first, no picking up a dropped tool. It was hard to pin down. One Sunday when Father, Betsie, and I were having dinner at Hilversum, I commented on what I had concluded was thoughtlessness.

Willem shook his head. "It's deliberate," he said. "It's because Christoffels is old. The old have no value to the State. They're also harder to train in the new ways of thinking. Germany is teaching disrespect for old age."

We could not grasp such a concept. "Surely you are mistaken, Willem!" Father said. "Otto is extremely courteous to me. And I'm a good deal older than Christoffels."

"You're the boss. That's another part of the system: respect for authority. The old and the weak are to be eliminated."

We started watching Otto more closely. But how could we know, how could we have guessed, that it was in the streets and alleys outside that Otto was subjecting Christoffels to very real persecution. "Accidental" trippings, a shove, a heel ground into a toe were making the old clockman's journeys to and from work times of terror.

Christoffels was too proud to report any of this to us. Only when one morning he stumbled into the dining room with a bleeding cheek did the truth come out. Even then, Christoffels said nothing. But running down the street to retrieve his hat, I encountered Otto surrounded by an indignant cluster of people who had seen what happened. The young man had forced the older one into the side of the building and ground his face against the rough bricks.

Father tried to reason with Otto as he let him go, to show him why such behavior was wrong. Otto did not answer. He collected the few tools he had brought with him and left the shop. At the door he turned to us briefly with a look of utter contempt.

5

INVASION

Father was eighty years old now, and promptly at 8:45 each evening he would open the Bible, read one chapter, ask God's blessing on us through the night, and by 9:15 be climbing the stairs to his bedroom. Tonight, however, the prime minister was to address the nation at 9:30. One question ached through all of Holland: Would there be war?

Father warmed up the radio. We did not spend evenings listening to music now. England, France, and Germany were at war, and even Dutch stations carried mostly war news. We could hear that news well enough on the small portable radio we kept in the dining room, a gift from Pickwick the Christmas before.

At 9:30 the prime minister's voice began. There would be no war. He had assurances from high sources on both sides.

Holland's neutrality would be respected. There was nothing to fear. Dutchmen were urged to remain calm—

The voice stopped. Betsie and I looked up. Father had snapped off the set, and in his blue eyes was a fire we had never seen before.

"It is wrong to give people hope when there is no hope," he said. "There will be war. The Germans will attack and we will fall."

His voice grew gentle again. "Oh, my dears, I am sorry for all Dutchmen now who do not know the power of God. For we will

be beaten. But He will not." He kissed us both good-night and then we heard him climb the stairs to bed.

Father, so skilled at finding good in every situation, so slow to believe evil. If Father saw war and defeat, then there was no other possibility.

I sat bolt upright in my bed. *What was that?* A brilliant flash followed a second later by an explosion that shook the bed. I scrambled to the window and leaned out. The patch of sky glowed orange-red.

I whirled down the stairs. At Father's room I pressed my ear against the door. Between bomb bursts I heard the regular rhythm of his breathing.

I dived down a few more steps and into Tante Jans' rooms. Betsie had moved into Tante Jans' sleeping cubicle to be closer to the kitchen and the doorbell. She was sitting up in bed.

Together we said it: "War."

It was five hours after the prime minister's speech. We tiptoed to Tante Jans' front room, where the glowing sky lit the room with a strange brilliance. Betsie and I knelt down for what seemed like hours, praying for our country, for the dead and injured tonight, for the queen. Then Betsie began to pray for the Germans, up there in the planes, caught in the evil loose in Germany. I looked at my sister kneeling beside me in the light of burning Holland. "Oh, Lord," I whispered, "listen to Betsie, not me, because I cannot pray for those men."

It was then that I had the dream. It could not have been a real dream, because I was not asleep. But a scene was suddenly and unreasonably in my mind. I clearly saw the Grote Markt, half a block away, saw the town hall and the fish mart. An old wagon came lumbering across the square pulled by four black horses. To my surprise I saw that I myself was sitting in the wagon. And Father, too! And Betsie! There were many others. I recognized Pickwick and Toos, Willem, and young Peter. Together we were slowly being drawn across the square behind those horses. The wagon was taking us away—far away, I felt—but we did not want to go. . . .

"Betsie!" I cried. "I've had an awful dream!"

I felt her arm around my shoulder. "We'll go make a pot of coffee."

The booming of the bombs was less frequent and farther away as Betsie put on the water. I told her what I had seen. "Am I imagining things? Was it a kind of vision?"

"I don't know," Betsie said softly. "But if God has shown us bad times ahead, it's enough for me that He knows about them. That's why He sometimes shows us things—to tell us that this, too, is in His hands."

For five days Holland held out against the invader. We kept the shop open, mostly because people wanted to see Father. Some wanted him to pray for husbands and sons stationed at the borders. Others, it seemed, came just to see him sitting there behind his workbench as he had for sixty years and to hear in those ticking clocks a world of order and reason.

I never opened my workbench, but joined Betsie in making coffee and carrying it down. We brought down the portable radio, too, and set it up. After that first night, although we often heard planes overhead, the bombing never came so close again.

Then the radio carried the news we dreaded: The queen had left. I did not cry the night of the invasion, but I cried now. In the morning the radio announced tanks advancing over the border.

Suddenly all of Haarlem was in the streets. Even Father, whose daily stroll was as predictable as his clocks, broke his routine to go walking at the unheard-of hour of 10:00 a.m. It was as though we wanted to face what was coming together, united. The three of us walked with the crowd in the street.

A window flew open. "We've surrendered!"

The walkers in the street stopped short. A boy of maybe fifteen turned to us with tears rolling down his cheeks. "I would have fought! I wouldn't ever have given up!" Father stooped down to pick up a small cherry blossom petal from the brick pavement; tenderly he inserted it in his buttonhole.

"That is good, my son," he told the youngster. "For Holland's battle has just begun."

During the first months of occupation, the hardest thing to get used to was the German uniform everywhere, German trucks and tanks in the street, German spoken in the shops. Soldiers frequently visited our store. They were getting good wages, and watches were among the first things they bought. Toward us they took a superior tone, but as I listened to them excitedly discussing their purchases to each other, they seemed like young men anywhere, selecting watches for mothers and sweethearts back home.

The shop never made as much money as during that first year of the war. With no new shipments coming in, people bought everything we had in stock.

The curfew, at first, was no hardship for us, since it was originally set at 10:00 p.m. What we did object to were the identity cards each citizen was issued. These small folders containing photograph and fingerprints had to be produced on demand. A soldier or a policeman—the Haarlem police were now under the control of the German commandant—might stop a citizen at any time and ask to see his card; it had to be carried in a pouch about the neck. We were issued ration cards, too.

Newspapers no longer carried news we could trust, only long glowing reports of the successes of the German army. So we depended on the radio.

Early in the occupation, Haarlemers were ordered to turn in all radios. Since it would look strange if our household produced none at all, Peter suggested we turn in the portable and hide the larger, more powerful instrument. Peter was sixteen at the time of the invasion and shared with other Dutch teenagers a restless energy. He installed the radio beneath a curve in the stairs just above Father's room and replaced the old boards, while I carried the smaller one down to where the radio collection was being made.

"Is this the only radio you own?" asked the army clerk.

I had known from childhood that the heavens rained fire upon liars, but I met his gaze.

"Yes."

I walked out of the building and began to tremble. For the first time in my life I had told a conscious lie. And it had been so easy.

But we had saved our radio. Every night one of us would remove the stair tread and crouch over the radio, the volume barely audible. Then one of us thumped the piano in Tante Jans' room as hard as she could. We listened to the news from England this way. The German offensive was everywhere victorious. Month after month the Free Dutch broadcasts could only urge us to wait, to have courage, to believe in the counter-offensive which must surely someday be mounted.

The Germans used our airport as a base for air raids against England. At night we heard the growl of engines heading west. Occasionally English planes retaliated, and then the German fighters might intercept them right over Haarlem.

One night as dogfights raged overhead, I heard Betsie stirring in the kitchen and ran down to join her. We went into the dining room, where we had covered the windows with heavy black paper. Somewhere in the night there was an explosion; the dishes in the cupboard rattled. We talked until the sound of planes died away and the sky was silent. I groped my way back up to my room.

I felt for my bed in the dark. My hand closed over something hard on my pillow. Sharp, too! I felt blood trickle along a finger.

It was a jagged piece of metal, ten inches long.

I raced down the stairs with the shrapnel shard in my hand. Betsie and I went back to the dining room and stared at it in the light while she bandaged my hand. "On your pillow," she kept saying.

"Betsie, if I hadn't heard you in the kitchen—"

Betsie put a finger on my mouth. "Don't say it, Corrie! There are no 'ifs' in God's world. The center of His will is our only safety. Oh, Corrie, let us pray that we may always know it!"

During the first year of German rule, there were only minor attacks on Jews in Holland—a rock through the window of a Jewish-owned store, an ugly word scrawled on the wall of a synagogue. It was as though they were testing to see how many Dutchmen would go along with them. The answer, to our shame, was many. The National Socialist Bond (NSB), Holland's organization of Nazi collaborators, grew larger and bolder with each month of occupation. Nazism was a disease to which some Dutch were susceptible.

On our daily walk, Father and I saw the symptoms spread. A sign in a shop window: Jews Will Not Be Served. At the entrance to a public park: No Jews. On the door of the library, in front of restaurants and theaters. A synagogue burned down and the fire trucks came—but only to keep the flames from spreading to the buildings on either side.

One noon as Father and I followed our familiar route, the sidewalks were bright with yellow stars sewn to coat and jacket fronts. Men, women, and children wore the six-pointed star with the word *Jood* (Jew) in the center. We were surprised to see how many of the people we passed each day were Jews.

Worst were the disappearances. Watches, repaired and ready, hung in the back of the shop, month after month. We never knew whether their owners had been spirited away by the Gestapo or had gone into hiding before this could happen.

One day as Father and I were returning from our walk, we found the Grote Markt cordoned off by a double ring of police and soldiers. Climbing into the back of a truck were men, women, and children, all wearing the yellow star.

"Father! Those poor people!" I cried.

The police line opened, and the truck moved through. We watched till it turned the corner.

"Those poor people," Father echoed. But to my surprise, he was looking at the soldiers. "I pity the poor Germans, Corrie. They have touched the apple of God's eye."

We talked often, Father, Betsie, and I, about what we could do if a chance should come to help some of our Jewish friends. We knew that Willem had found hiding places at the beginning of the occupation for the German Jews who had been living in his house. Willem would be the one to ask.

On a drizzly November morning in 1941, a year and a half after the invasion, I stepped outside to fold back the shutters. I saw four German soldiers coming down the Barteljorisstraat, combat helmets low over their ears, rifles strapped to their shoulders. I shrank back and watched. At Weil's Furriers, directly across the street, the group stopped. One of the soldiers unstrapped his gun and with the butt banged on the door. The door opened and all four pushed inside.

I dashed back through our shop and up to the dining room. "Betsie! Hurry! Something awful is happening at Weil's!" We reached the front door in time to see Mr. Weil backing out of his shop, the muzzle of a gun pressed against his stomach. The soldier left him on the sidewalk, went back into the store, and slammed the door.

We could hear glass breaking inside. Soldiers began carrying out armloads of furs. A crowd was gathering in spite of the early morning hour. Mr. Weil had not moved from his spot on the sidewalk.

A window over his head opened and a shower of clothes rained down on him—pajamas, shirts, underwear. Slowly, the old furrier began to gather up his clothing. Betsie and I ran across the street to help him.

"Your wife!" Betsie whispered. "Where is Mrs. Weil?"

The man blinked at her.

"You must come inside!" I said, snatching socks and handkerchiefs from the sidewalk. We propelled the bewildered man across to the Beje. In the dining room, Father greeted Mr. Weil without the slightest sign of surprise. His natural manner seemed to relax the furrier a bit. His wife, he said, was visiting a sister in Amsterdam.

"We must warn her not to come home!" Betsie said.

Where were the Weils to live? Father and Betsie and I exchanged glances. *Willem.*

Someone had to go talk to Willem. It was not the kind of matter that could be relayed through the public phone system, and like most private telephones, ours had been disconnected early in the occupation.

I went by train. When I reached the nursing home, Willem was not there. But Tine and their 22-year-old son, Kik, were. I told them what had happened.

"Tell Mr. Weil to be ready as soon as it's dark," Kik said.

At nearly 9:00 p.m.—the new curfew hour—Kik rapped at the alley door. Tucking Mr. Weil's clothing bundle beneath his arm, he led the man away into the night.

Two weeks later I saw Kik and asked him what had happened. He smiled at me, the broad, slow smile I had loved since he was a child. "If you're going to work with the underground, Tante Corrie, you must learn not to ask questions."

Kik's words went round and round in my head: *"If you're going to work with the underground . . ."* Was Kik working with this secret and illegal group? Was Willem?

We suspected, of course, that there was an underground in Holland. Rumors abounded. The stories always featured things we believed were wrong in the sight of God. Stealing, lying, murder. Was this what God wanted in times like these? How should a Christian act when evil was in power?

Father now housed in Tanta Jans' big mahogany bookcases a large collection of Jewish theology, belonging to the rabbi of Haarlem. He had brought them to Father more than a year before: "Just in case I should not be able to care for them . . . ah . . . indefinitely." He had waved apologetically at the procession of small boys behind him, each staggering under the weight of several huge volumes. "Books do not age as you and I do, old friend. They will speak when we are gone, to generations we will never see. The books must survive."

The rabbi had been one of the first to vanish from Haarlem.

As arrests of Jews in the street became more frequent, I began picking up and delivering work for our Jewish customers myself so that they would not have to venture into the center of town. One evening in the spring of 1942, I was in the home of a doctor and his wife. The Heemstras and I were talking about the news of the day, when down the stairs piped a childish voice.

"Daddy! You didn't tuck us in!"

Dr. Heemstra was on his feet in an instant. With an apology to his wife and me, he hurried upstairs, and in a minute we heard a game of hide-and-seek going and the laughter of two children.

In that instant, reality broke through the numbness that had grown in me since the invasion. At any minute there might be a rap on this door. These children, this mother and father, might be ordered to the back of a truck.

Dr. Heemstra came back to the living room, and the conversation rambled on. But a prayer was forming in my heart. *Lord Jesus, I offer myself for Your people. In any way. Any place. Any time.*

Again, that waking dream passed before my eyes. I saw those four black horses and the Grote Markt. As I had on the night of the invasion, I scanned the passengers. Father, Betsie, Willem, myself—leaving Haarlem, leaving all that was sure and safe—going where?

6

THE SECRET ROOM

Each month, the occupation seemed to grow harsher, restrictions more numerous. The latest heartache for Dutchmen was an edict making it a crime to sing the "Wilhelmus," our national anthem.

On a Sunday two years after the occupation, Father, Betsie, and I were on our way to church in a small town where Peter had won the post of organist. The organ at Velsen was one of the finest in the country.

Peter was already playing in the tall organ loft when we squeezed into the crowded pew. That was one thing the occupation had done for Holland: Churches were packed.

After closing prayers were said, suddenly, electrically, the whole church sat at attention. Without preamble, every stop pulled out to full volume, Peter was playing the "Wilhelmus"!

Father, at 82, was the first one on his feet. Now everyone stood. From somewhere in back of us a voice sang out the words. Another joined in, and another. We were all singing together at the top of our lungs our forbidden anthem.

Afterward we waited for Peter at the small side door of the church while people embraced him or shook his hand. But now that the moment had passed, I was angry with him. The Gestapo was certain to hear about it. I thought of Nollie, home fixing Sunday dinner for us all. I thought of Peter's brothers and sisters. And what if Flip lost the principalship of the school for this? For what had Peter risked so much, for a moment's defiance?

At his home, however, Peter was a hero. The only members of the household who felt as I did were the two Jewish women staying at Nollie's. One of these was an elderly lady whom Willem had sent into hiding there. "Katrien," as the family had rechristened her, was posing as the von Woerden's housemaid.

The other woman was a young, blond, blue-eyed Dutch Jew with flawless false identity papers supplied by the Dutch underground. The papers were so good and Annaliese looked so unlike the Nazi stereotype of a Jew that she went freely in and out of the house, pretending to be a friend of the family whose husband had died. Katrien and Annaliese could not understand any more than I could Peter doing something that would attract the attention of the authorities.

On Wednesday morning just as Father and I were unlocking our workbenches, Peter's little sister Cocky burst into the shop.

"They came for Peter! They took him away!"

He had been taken to prison in Amsterdam.

One evening two weeks later, Father and Betsie and I were seated around the dining room table, Father replacing watches in their pockets and Betsie doing needlework. A knock on the alley door made me glance in the win-  dow mirror. There in the spring twilight stood a woman. She carried a small suitcase and—odd for the time of year—wore a fur coat and gloves.

I ran down and opened the door. "Can I come in?" she asked. Her voice was high-pitched in fear.

"Of course." I stepped back. The woman looked over her shoulder before moving into the little hallway.

"My name is Kleermaker. I'm a Jew."

"How do you do? Won't you come upstairs?"

Father and Betsie stood up as we entered the dining room. "Mrs. Kleermaker, my father and my sister."

Father drew out a chair from the table, and Mrs. Kleermaker sat down, still gripping her suitcase. She plunged into the story of how her husband had been arrested some months before and her son had gone into hiding. Yesterday the S.D.—the police who worked under the Gestapo—had ordered her to close the family store. She was afraid now to go back to the apartment above it.

"In this household," Father said, "God's people are always welcome."

Just two nights later, the same scene was repeated: a furtive knock at the side door and this time an elderly couple standing outside. It was the same story, the same tight-clutched possessions, the same fearful glance. The story of neighbors arrested, the fear that tomorrow their turn would come.

The next day I made the trip to Hilversum. "Willem," I said, "we have three Jews staying right at the Beje. Can you get places for them in the country?"

"It's getting harder," Willem said. "They're feeling the food shortage even on the farms. I still have addresses, but they won't take anyone without a ration card."

"But Jews aren't issued ration cards!"

For the first time I wondered how he and Tine were feeding the elderly men and women in their care.

Willem continued: "I know. And ration cards can't be counterfeited. They're changed too often and they're too easy to spot. Identity cards are different. I know several printers who do them. Of course, you need a photographer."

A photographer? Printers? What was Willem talking about? "Willem, if people need ration cards and there aren't any counterfeit ones, what do you do?"

Willem gestured vaguely. "Steal them."

I stared at this Dutch Reformed clergyman. "Then, Willem, could you steal . . . I mean . . . could you get three stolen cards?"

"No, Corrie! Every move I make is watched!" He put an arm around my shoulder. "It will be far better for you to develop

63

your own sources. The less connection with me—the less connection with anyone else—the better."

On the crowded train home, I turned Willem's words over in my mind. *Your own sources.* That sounded so . . . professional. How was I going to find a source of stolen ration cards? Who in the world did I know . . .?

A name appeared in my mind.

Fred Koornstra was the man who used to read the electric meter at the Beje. Now Fred had a job working for the Food Office. Wasn't it in the department where ration books were issued?

That evening after supper I bumped over the brick streets to the Koornstra house. The tires on my bicycle had finally given out, and I had joined the hundreds clattering about town on metal wheel rims.

Fred came to the door and stared at me blankly when I said I wanted to talk to him about the Sunday service. He invited me in, closed the door, and said, "Now, what did you really come to see me about?"

Lord, I prayed silently, *if it is not safe to confide in Fred, stop this conversation now before it is too late.*

"We've had some unexpected company at the Beje. First it was a single woman, then a couple, and when I got back this afternoon, another couple." I paused for an instant. "They are Jews."

Fred's expression did not change.

I continued. "We can find safe places for them, but they must provide something too. Ration cards."

Fred's eyes smiled. "Now I know why you came here."

"Is there any way you can give out extra cards? More than you report?"

"No, Corrie. Those cards have to be accounted for a dozen ways. They're checked and double-checked."

The hope in me began to tumble. But Fred was frowning. "Unless . . ." he began, "there were a hold-up. The Food Office in Utrecht was robbed last month—but the men were caught."

He was silent a while. "If it happened at noon," he said slowly, "when just the record clerk and I are there . . . and if they found us tied and gagged . . ." He snapped his fingers. "I know just the man who might do it! Do you remember the—"

"Don't!" I said, remembering Willem's warning. "Don't tell me who or how. Just get the cards if you possibly can."

"How many do you need?"

I opened my mouth to say "Five." But the number that astonishingly came out instead was "One hundred."

When Fred opened the door to me just a week later, I gasped at the sight of him. Both eyes were a greenish purple, his lower lip cut and swollen.

"My friend took very naturally to the part," was all he would say.

On the table in a brown manila envelope were one hundred ration cards. Fred had already torn the "continuing coupon" from each one. This final coupon was presented at the Food Office the last day of each month in exchange for the next month's card. With these coupons Fred could "legally" continue to issue us one hundred cards.

We agreed that it would be risky for me to keep coming to his house each month. What if he were to come to the Beje instead, dressed in his old meterman uniform?

The meter in the Beje was in the back hall at the foot of the stairs. When I got home that afternoon, I pried up the tread of the bottom step and found a hollow space inside.

We soon had our first test of the system. Fred was to come in through the shop as he always had, carrying the cards beneath his shirt. He would come at 5:30, when Betsie would have the back hall free of callers. To my horror at 5:25 the shop door opened and in stepped a policeman.

He was a tall man with orange-red hair whom I knew by name—Rolf—but little else. He had come to the hundredth birthday party, but so had half the force.

Rolf brought in a watch that needed cleaning, and he seemed in a mood to talk. My throat went dry, but Father chatted cheerfully as he took off the back of Rolf's watch and examined it. What were we going to do? There was no way to warn Fred Koornstra. Promptly at 5:30 the door of the shop opened and in he walked, dressed in his blue workclothes. It seemed to me that his chest was too thick by a foot at least.

Fred nodded to Father, the policeman, and me. "Good evening." He strode through the door at the rear of the shop and shut it behind him. My ears strained to hear him. The door behind us opened again. So great was Fred's control that he had not ducked out the alleyway exit, but came strolling back through the shop.

"Good evening," he said again.

He reached the street door and was gone. We got away with it this time, but we were going to have to work out a warning system.

Meanwhile a great deal had happened at the Beje. Supplied with ration cards, Mrs. Kleermaker and the elderly couple and the next arrivals and the next had found homes in safer locations. Still the hunted people kept coming, and the needs were often more complicated than ration cards and addresses. If a Jewish woman became pregnant, where could she go to have her baby? If a Jew in hiding died, how could he be buried?

"Develop your own sources," Willem had said. From the moment Fred Koornstra's name had popped into my mind, an uncanny realization had been growing in me. We were friends with half of Haarlem! We knew someone in every business and service in the city.

We did not know the political views of all these people. But—and here I felt a strange leaping of my heart—God did! My job was simply to follow His leading, holding every decision up to Him in prayer. I knew I was not clever or sophisticated; if the Beje was becoming a meeting place for need and supply, it was through some strategy far higher than mine.

A few nights after Fred's first "meterman" visit, the alley bell rang long after curfew. I sped downstairs expecting another refugee.

To my surprise, close against the wall of the dark alley, stood Kik. "Get your bicycle," he ordered with his usual abruptness.

"And put on a sweater. I have some people I want you to meet."
I knew it was useless to ask questions.

Kik's bicycle was tireless, too, the wheel rims swathed in
cloth. He wrapped mine also to keep down the clatter, and soon
we were pedaling through the blacked-out streets of Haarlem
at a speed that would have scared me even in daylight.

"Put a hand on my shoulder," Kik whispered. "I know the
way."

We crossed dark side streets, crested bridges, wheeled around
corners. At last we crossed a broad canal and into the fashion-
able suburb Aerdenhout.

We turned into a driveway beneath shadowy trees. To my
astonishment, Kik picked up my bicycle and carried both his
and mine up the front steps. A serving girl with starched white
apron and ruffled cap opened the door.
The entrance hall was jammed
with bicycles.

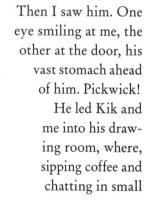

Then I saw him. One
eye smiling at me, the
other at the door, his
vast stomach ahead
of him. Pickwick!
He led Kik and
me into his draw-
ing room, where,
sipping coffee and
chatting in small

groups, was the most distinguished-looking group of men and women I had ever seen. But all my attention, that first moment, was on the fragrant aroma in that room. Was it possible they were drinking real coffee?

Pickwick drew me a cup from the silver urn on the sideboard. It was indeed coffee. After two years, here was rich, black, pungent Dutch coffee. He poured himself a cup, too, dropping in his usual five lumps of sugar as though rationing had never been invented. Another starched and ruffled maid passed a tray heaped high with cakes.

Gobbling and gulping, I trailed about the room after Pickwick, shaking the hands of the people he singled out. They were strange introductions, for no names were mentioned, only, occasionally, an address, and "Ask for Mrs. Smit." When I had met my fourth Smit, Kik explained with a grin, "It's the only last name in the underground."

So this was the underground! But where were these people from? I had never laid eyes on any of them. Eventually I realized with a shiver down my spine that I was meeting the national group.

Their chief work, I learned from bits of conversation, was liaison with England and the Free Dutch forces fighting elsewhere on the continent. They also maintained the underground route through which downed Allied plane crews reached the North Sea coast.

They were instantly sympathetic with my efforts to help Haarlem's Jews. I blushed to hear Pickwick describe me as "the head of an operation in this city." A hollow space under the stairs and some haphazard friendships were not an operation. The others here were obviously professional.

But they greeted me with grave courtesy, murmuring what they had to offer. False identity papers. The use of a car with official government plates. Signature forgery.

In a far corner of the room Pickwick introduced me to a little man with a wispy goatee. "Our host informs me," the man began formally, "that your headquarters building lacks a secret room. This is a danger for all. With your permission I will pay you a visit in the coming week." Years later I would learn that he was one of the most famous architects in Europe. I knew him only as Mr. Smit.

Just before Kik and I started our dash back to the Beje, Pickwick slipped an arm through mine. "My dear, I have good news. I understand that Peter is about to be released."

So he was, three days later, thinner, paler, and not a whit daunted by his two months in a concrete cell. We used up a month's sugar ration baking cakes for his welcome-home party.

One morning soon afterward, the first customer in the shop was a small thin-bearded man named Smit. Father took his jeweler's glass from his eye. If there was one thing he loved better than making a new acquaintance, it was discovering a link with an old one.

"Smit," he said. "I know several Smits in Amsterdam. Are you by any chance related to the family who—"

"Father," I interrupted, "this is the man I told you about. He's come to inspect the house."

"A building inspector? Then you must be the Smit with offices in the Grote Hout Straat."

"Father!" I pleaded. "He's not a building inspector, and his name is not Smit."

As I led Mr. Smit into the back hall, we heard Father musing to himself, "I once knew a Smit on Koning Straat. . . ."

Mr. Smit examined and approved the hiding place for ration cards beneath the bottom step. He also pronounced acceptable the warning system we had worked out. This was a triangle-shaped wooden sign advertising Alpina Watches that I had placed in the dining room window. As long as the sign was in place, it was safe to enter.

But when I showed him a cubby hole behind the corner cupboard in the dining room, he shook his head. Some ancient redesigning of the house had left a crawl space in that corner, and we had been secreting jewelry, silver coins, and other valuables there. Not only had the rabbi brought us his library, but other Jewish families had brought their treasures to the Beje for safekeeping. The space was large enough that we believed a person could crawl in there if necessary, but Mr. Smit dismissed it without a second glance.

"First place they'd look. Don't bother to change it, though. It's only silver. We're interested in saving people, not things."

He started up the narrow corkscrew stairs, and as he mounted so did his spirits. He paused in delight at the odd-placed landings, pounded on the crooked walls, and laughed aloud as the floor levels of the two old houses continued out of phase.

"What an impossibility!" he said in an awestruck voice. "What an unbelievable, unpredictable impossibility! Miss ten Boom, if all houses were constructed like this one, you would see before you a less worried man."

At the top of the stairs, he entered my bedroom. "This is it!" he exclaimed. "You want your hiding place as high as possible. Gives you the best chance to reach it while the search is on below."

Mr. Smit began measuring. He moved the wobbly old wardrobe away from the wall and pulled my bed into the center of the room. "This is where the false wall will go!" Excitedly he penciled a line along the floor thirty inches from the back wall. He stood up and gazed at it.

"That's as big as I dare," he said. "It will easily take a cot mattress, though."

Over the next few days, Mr. Smit and his workmen were in and out of our house. They never knocked. At each visit each man carried in something. Tools in a folded newspaper. A few bricks in a briefcase.

I ventured to wonder if a wooden wall would not be easier to build.

"Wood sounds hollow," he said. "No. Brick's the only thing for false walls."

After the wall was up, the plasterer came, then the carpenter, finally the painter. Six days after he had begun, Mr. Smit called Father, Betsie, and me to see.

We stood in the doorway and gaped. The smell of fresh paint was everywhere. But surely nothing in this room was newly painted! All four walls had that streaked and grimy look that old rooms got in coal-burning Haarlem. The ancient molding ran unbroken around the ceiling, chipped and peeling here and there, obviously undisturbed for 150 years. Old water stains streaked the back wall—a wall that even I, who had lived half a century in this room, could scarcely believe was not the original, but set back a precious two-and-a-half feet from the true wall of the building.

Built-in bookshelves, old, sagging shelves with the same water stains as the wall behind them, ran along this false wall.

Down in the far lefthand corner, beneath the bottom shelf, a sliding panel, two feet high and two wide, opened into the secret room.

Mr. Smit stooped and pulled this panel up. On hands and knees, Betsie and I crawled into the narrow room behind it. Inside we could stand up, sit, or even stretch out one at a time on the single mattress. A concealed vent allowed air to enter from outside.

"Keep a water jug there," said Mr. Smit, crawling in behind us. "Change the water once a week. Hardtack and vitamins keep indefinitely. Anytime there is anyone in the house whose presence is unofficial, all possessions except the clothes on his back must be stored in here."

Dropping to our knees again, we crawled out single file. "Move back into your bedroom," he told me. "Everything exactly as before."

With his fist he struck the wall above the bookshelves. "The Gestapo could search for a year," he said. "They'll never find this one."

7

EUSIE

Peter was home, yet he was not safe, any more than any healthy young male was safe. In Germany the munitions factories were desperate for workers. Without warning, soldiers would suddenly surround a block of buildings and sweep through them, herding every male between sixteen and thirty into trucks for transport. This method of lightning search and seizure was called the *razzia*, and every family with young men lived in dread of it.

Flip and Nollie rearranged their kitchen to give them an emergency hiding place as soon as the razzias started. There was a small potato cellar beneath the kitchen floor. They enlarged the trapdoor letting into it, put a large rug on top of it, and moved the kitchen table to stand on this spot.

Since Mr. Smit's work at the Beje, I realized that this hole under the kitchen floor was an inadequate hiding place and probably, as Mr. Smit would say, "the first place they'd look." However, it was planned not for a sustained search by trained officials, but a swoop by soldiers, a place to get out of sight for half an hour. For that, it was probably sufficient.

It was Flip's birthday when the razzia came to that quiet residential street. Father, Betsie, and I had come early. Nollie, Annaliese, and the two older girls were out when we arrived.

We were chatting in the kitchen with Cocky and Katrien when all at once Peter and his older brother, Bob, raced into the room, their faces white. "Soldiers! They're two doors down and coming this way!"

They jerked the table back, snatched away the rug, and tugged open the trapdoor. Bob lowered himself first, lying down flat, and Peter tumbled in on top of him. We dropped the door shut, yanked the rug over it, and pulled the table back in place. With trembling hands, Betsie, Cocky, and I threw a long tablecloth over it and started laying five places for tea.

There was a crash in the hall as the front door burst open and a smaller crash as Cocky dropped a teacup. Two uniformed Germans ran into the kitchen, rifles leveled.

"Stay where you are."

We heard boots storming up the stairs. The soldiers glanced around at this room filled with women and one old man.

"Where are your men?" the shorter soldier asked Cocky.

"These are my aunts," she said, "and this is my grandfather. My father is at his school, and my mother is shopping, and—"

"I didn't ask about the whole tribe!" the man exploded in German. Then in Dutch: "Where are your brothers?"

Cocky stared at him a second. My heart stood still. I knew how Nollie had trained her children—but surely now of all times a lie was permissible!

"Do you have brothers?" the officer asked again.

"Yes," Cocky said softly. "Three."

"How old are they?"

"Twenty-one, nineteen, and eighteen."

Upstairs we heard the sounds of doors opening and shutting, the scrape of furniture dragged from walls.

"Where are they now?" the soldier persisted.

Cocky leaned down and began gathering up the broken bits of cup. The man jerked her upright. "Where are your brothers?"

"The oldest one is at the Theological College."

"What about the other two?"

Cocky did not miss a breath. "They're under the table."

Motioning us all away with his gun, the soldier seized a corner of the tablecloth and flung it back.

Suddenly Cocky burst into spasms of hysterical laughter. The soldiers whirled around. Was she laughing at them?

"Don't take us for fools!" the short one snarled. Furiously he strode from the room, and minutes later the entire squad trooped out.

It was a strange dinner party that evening, veering as it did from heartfelt thanksgiving to the nearest thing to a bitter argument our close-knit family ever had. Nollie stuck by Cocky, insisting she would have answered the same way. "God honors truth-telling with perfect protection!"

Peter and Bob, from the viewpoint of the trapdoor, were not so sure. And neither was I. I had never had Nollie's bravery— nor her faith. But I could spot illogic. "It isn't logical to *say* the truth and *do* a lie! What about Annaliese's false papers—and that maid's uniform on Katrien?"

"'Set a watch, O Lord, before my mouth,'" Nollie quoted. "'Keep the door of my lips.' Psalm 141!"

"All right, what about the radio? I had to lie with my lips to keep that!"

"Whatever came from your lips, Corrie, I am sure it was spoken in love!" Father's kindly voice reproached my flushed face.

Love. How did one show it? How could God Himself show truth and love at the same time in a world like this?

By dying. The answer stood out for me sharper and chillier than it ever had before that night: the shape of a Cross etched on the history of the world.

By early 1943, it was getting harder to find safe homes in the country for the scores of Jews who were passing through our underground station. Even with ration cards and forged papers, there were not enough places for them all. Sooner or later we knew we were going to have to start hiding people in the city.

That year winter came cold and early and stayed late. Fuel was scarce. In parks and along the canals, trees began to disappear as people cut them down to burn for heat.

One morning Christoffels did not show for work, and his landlady found him dead in his bed. We buried the old clockmaker in the splendid suit and vest he had worn to the hundredth birthday party, six years and another lifetime ago.

Spring came slowly. I celebrated my 51st birthday. A couple of weeks after, we were helped with a reunion of a married

Jewish couple by the red-haired policeman named Rolf. We were surprised and grateful for his help, and that night we held a meeting about him: Betsie and I and the dozen or so teenage boys and girls who acted as messengers for this work. If Rolf had risked his own safety to help us, perhaps he should work with us.

"Lord Jesus," I said aloud, "this could be a danger for all of us and for Rolf, too." But even with the words came a flood of assurance about this man. How long, I wondered, would we be led by this gift of knowledge.

I assigned one of our younger boys to follow Rolf home from work the next day and learn where he lived. The older boys, those susceptible to the factory draft, we sent out only after dark now and most often dressed as girls.

The following week I visited Rolf at home. "You have no idea how much your help meant to us," I said when I was inside. "How can we repay this kindness?"

Rolf ran his hands through his bright hair. "Well, there is a way. The cleaning woman at the jail has a teenage son, and they've almost picked him up twice. She's desperate to find another place for him to live."

"Perhaps I can help," I said. "Do you think she could find that her watch needs repairing?"

The next day Toos came to me. "There's a funny looking little woman downstairs," Toos said. "Her name is Mietje. She says to tell you Rolf sent her."

I met Mietje in the dining room. The hand that I shook was ridged and leathery from years of scrubbing floors. "I understand," I said, "that you have a son you're very proud of."

"Oh, yes!" Mietje's face lit up at the mention of him.

I took the alarm clock she had brought with her. "Come for your clock tomorrow afternoon and I'll hope to have good news."

That night we learned there was a place available on a nearby tulip farm, but the farmer had decided he must be paid for the risk he was taking. We would have to provide a fee plus an additional ration card. It did not happen often that a "host" would require money for his services; when one did we paid gladly.

When Mietje appeared the following morning, I took a small banknote from my purse and tore off a corner. "This is for your son," I said. "Tonight he is to go to the Gravenstenenbrug. There is a tree stump next to the bridge. He is to wait beside it, looking into the canal. A man will come up and ask if he has change for a bankbill. Your son is to match the missing corner, and then follow this man without asking questions."

Mietje grasped my hand in her two sandpaper ones. "Someday, I'll find a way to repay you!"

I smiled. How could this simple soul help with the kind of need we faced?

So the work grew. As each new need arose, a new answer was found, too. Through Pickwick, for example, we met the man at the central telephone exchange whose department handled orders to connect and disconnect lines. With a little rewiring and juggling of numbers, he soon had our instrument in operation.

What a day it was when the old wall phone in the rear hall jangled for the first time in three years! And how we needed it! By now there were eighty Dutchmen—elderly women and middle-aged men along with our teenagers—working in "God's underground" as we sometimes laughingly called ourselves.

Most of these people never saw one another; we kept face-to-face contacts as few as possible. But all knew the Beje. It was headquarters, the center of a spreading web.

But the telephone was also a fresh risk. We set the phone's ring as low as we could and still hear it; but who might be passing through the hall when it rang? For that matter, how long would curious eyes up and down the street continue to believe that one small watch shop was quite as busy as it appeared? It was true that repair work was in demand; plenty of legitimate customers passed in and out. But there was too much coming and going, especially in the early evening, and curfew was now 7:00 p.m.

We could never be sure our line was not tapped. So we developed a system for coding our underground messages in terms of watches.

"We have a woman's watch here that needs repairing. But I can't find a mainspring. Do you know who might have one?" (We have a Jewish woman in need of a hiding place, and we cannot find one among our regular contacts.)

"I have a watch here with a face that's causing difficulty. One of the numbers has worked loose, and it's holding back the hand. Do you know anyone who does this kind of repair work?" (We have a Jew here whose features are especially Semitic. Do you know anyone who would be willing to take an extra risk?)

"I'm sorry, but the watch you left with us is not repairable. Do you have the receipt?" (A Jew has died in one of our houses. We need a burial permit.)

One morning in the middle of June, the telephone rang with this message: "We have a man's watch here that's giving us trouble. We can't find anyone to repair it. For one thing, the face is very old-fashioned. . . ."

So, a Jew whose features gave him away. This was the hardest kind of person to place. "Send the watch over and I'll see what we can do in our own shop," I said.

Promptly at 7:00 that evening the side doorbell rang. I glanced at the mirror in the window of the dining room, where we were still sitting. Even from the side of his head I could tell that this was our old-fashioned watch.

I ran down to the door. "Do come in."

The smiling man in his early thirties, with a balding head and minuscule glasses, gave an elaborate bow. I liked him instantly.

Once the door was closed, he took out a pipe. "The very first thing I must ask," he said, "is whether or not I should leave behind my good friend the pipe? Meyer Mossel and his pipe are not easily separated. But for you, kind lady, I would gladly say good-bye to my friend."

I laughed. Of all who had come to our house, this was the first to enter cheerfully and with a question about our comfort.

"Keep your pipe!" I said.

I took him up to the dining room. There were seven seated at the table, a Jewish couple waiting placement and three underground workers in addition to Father and Betsie. Meyer Mossel's eyes went straight to Father.

"But," he cried, "one of the Patriarchs!"

It was exactly the right thing to say to Father. "But," he returned with equal good humor, "a brother of the Chosen People!"

"Can you recite the 166th Psalm, Opa?" Meyer said.

Father beamed. Of course there is no Psalm 166; the Psalter stops with 150. It must be a joke, and nothing could please Father better than a scriptural joke.

"Shall I recite it for you?" Meyer asked.

Father gave a bow of assent and Meyer plunged into verse.

"But that's Psalm 100!" Father interrupted. Then his face lit up. Of course! Psalm 66 started with the identical words. Meyer had asked for the 100th *and* the 66th Psalm. For the rest of the evening I could hear Father chuckling, "Psalm 166!"

At 8:45 Father took the Bible from its shelf. He opened to the reading in Jeremiah where we had left off the night before, then passed the Bible across the table to Meyer.

"I would consider it an honor if you would read tonight," Father said.

Lifting the Book lovingly, Meyer rose to his feet. From a pocket came a small prayer cap, and then, from deep in this throat, half-sung, half-pleaded, came the words of the ancient prophet.

We would learn he had been cantor in the synagogue in Amsterdam. For all his lightheartedness he had suffered much. Most of his family had been arrested; his wife and children were in hiding on a farm that had declined to accept Meyer—"For obvious reasons," he said with a grimace.

Gradually it dawned on us that this endearing man was at the Beje to stay. It was certainly not an ideal place, but for Meyer nothing could be ideal right now.

"At least," I told him one evening as we sat with Kik and others around the table, "your name doesn't have to give you away, too. I think we'll call you Eusebius."

Meyer leaned back and took his pipe out of his mouth. "Eusebius Mossel," he said. "It doesn't sound quite right."

We all laughed. Kik looked slyly at Father. "Opa! How about Smit? That seems a popular name these days."

"It does seem so!" said Father, not catching the joke.

And Eusebius Smit he became, affectionately called "Eusie."

Within a week there were three new permanent additions to the household. First there was Jop, our current apprentice, whose daily trip from his parents' home in the suburbs had twice nearly ended in seizure for the factory transport. The second time it happened his parents asked if he could stay at the Beje and we agreed. The other two were Henk, a young lawyer, and Leendert, a schoolteacher. Leendert made an especially important contribution to the secret life of the Beje. He installed our electric warning system.

By now I had learned to make the nighttime trip out to Pickwick's almost as skillfully as could Kik. One evening when I had gratefully accepted a cup of coffee, my friend sat me down for a lecture.

"Cornelia," he said, "I understand you have no alarm system in your house. This is purest folly. Also I am given to believe that you are not carrying on regular drills for your guests."

I was always amazed at how well Pickwick knew what went on at the Beje.

"A raid may come any day," Pickwick continued. "I don't see how you can avoid one. Scores of people in and out—and an NSB agent living up the street. Your secret room is no good to you if people can't get to it in time. I know this Leendert. He's a very passable electrician. Get him to put a buzzer in every room with a door or a window on the street. Then hold practice drills until your people can disappear in that room without a trace in less than a minute."

Leendert did the electrical work that weekend. He installed a buzzer near the top of the stairs—loud enough to be heard all over the house but not outside. Then he placed buttons to sound the buzzer at every vantage point where trouble might first be spotted. One button went beneath the dining room windowsill. Another went in the downstairs hall just inside that door, and a third inside the front door. He also put a button behind the counter in the shop and one in each workbench as well as beneath the windows in Tante Jans' rooms.

We were ready for our first trial run. The four unacknowledged members of our household were already climbing up to the secret room two times a day: in the morning to store their night clothes, bedding, and toilet articles, and in the evening to put away their day things. Members of our group who had to spend the night also kept raincoats, hats, anything they had brought with them in that room. That made a good deal of traffic in and out of my small bedroom—smaller now by nearly a yard. Many nights my last waking sight would be Eusie in robe and tasseled nightcap, handing his day clothes through the secret panel.

But the purpose of the drills was to see how rapidly people could reach the room at any hour of the day or night without prior notice. A tall young man arrived from Pickwick one morning to teach me how to conduct the drills.

"Smit!" Father exclaimed when the man introduced himself. "Truly it's most astonishing! We've had one Smit after another here lately."

Mr. Smit disentangled himself gently from Father's inquiries and followed me upstairs.

"Mealtimes," he said. "That's a favorite hour for a raid. Also the middle of the night." He strode from room to room, pointing to evidence that more than three people lived in the house. He paused in a bedroom door. "If the raid comes at night, they must not only take their sheets and blankets but get the mattress turned. That's the S.D.'s favorite trick—feeling for a warm spot on a bed."

Mr. Smit stayed for lunch. There were eleven of us at the table that day, including a Jewish lady who had arrived the night before and a Gentile woman and her small daughter, members of our underground, who acted as "escorts." The three of them were leaving for a farm right after lunch.

Betsie had just passed around a stew so artfully prepared you scarcely missed the meat when, without warning, Mr. Smit leaned back in his chair and pushed the button below the window.

Above us the buzzer sounded. People sprang to their feet, snatching up glasses and plates, scrambling for the stairs. Cries of "Faster!" "Not so loud!" and "You're spilling it!" reached us as Father, Betsie, and I hastily rearranged table and chairs to look like a lunch for three in progress.

"No, leave my place," Mr. Smit instructed. "Why shouldn't you have a guest for lunch? The lady and the little girl could have stayed, too."

At last we were seated again and silence reigned upstairs. The whole process had taken four minutes.

Later we gathered again around the dining room table. Mr. Smit set out before him the incriminating evidence he had found: two spoons and a piece of carrot on the stairs, pipe ashes in an "unoccupied" bedroom.

The next night I sounded the alarm again, and this time we shaved a minute and 33 seconds off our run. By our fifth trial we were down to two minutes. We never did achieve Pickwick's ideal of under a minute, but with practice we learned to jump up from whatever we were doing and get those who had to hide into the secret room in seventy seconds. Father, Toos, and I worked on "stalling techniques," which we would use if the Gestapo came through the shop door; Betsie invented a similar strategy for the side door. With those delaying tactics, we hoped we could gain life-saving seconds.

Soon we had three more permanent boarders arrive: Thea Dacosta, Meta Monsanto, and Mary Itallie. The moment Mary stepped through our door, I heard the asthmatic wheezing that had made other hosts unwilling to take her in.

Since her ailment compromised the safety of the others, we gathered in Tante Jans' front room—Eusie, Jop, Henk, Leendert, Meta, Thea, and Mary herself joined Father, Betsie, and me.

"There is no sense in pretending," I began. "Mary has a difficulty that could put you all in danger." In the silence that followed, Mary's labored breathing seemed especially loud.

Eusie spoke first. "It seems to me that we're all here in your house because we're the ones nobody else wanted. Any one of us is jeopardizing the others. I vote that Mary stay."

"Good," said lawyer Henk. "Let's put it to the vote."

Hands began rising, but Mary struggled to speak. "Secret ballots," she said at last. "No one should be embarrassed."

Henk tore a sheet of paper into nine strips. "You too," he said, handing ballots to Betsie, Father, and me. "If we're discovered, you suffer, too."

He handed around pencils. "Mark no if it's too great a risk, yes if you think she belongs here."

For a moment pencils scratched, and then Henk collected the folded ballots. He opened them in silence, then reached over and dropped them into Mary's lap.

Nine scraps of paper, nine times the word yes.

So our "family" was formed. Others stayed with us a day or a week, but these seven remained, the nucleus of our happy household. That it could have been happy, at such a time and in such circumstances, was largely a tribute to Betsie. Because our guests' lives were so restricted, evenings under Betsie's direction became the door to the wide world. Sometimes we had concerts, with Leendert on the violin and Thea on the piano. Or Betsie would announce a title of a play with each of us reading a part. One night a week she talked Eusie into giving Hebrew lessons, another night Meta taught Italian.

The city now had electricity only a brief time each night, and candles were hoarded for emergencies. When the lamps dimmed, we would go back down to the dining room, where my bicycle was set up on its stand. While the others took chairs, one of us would climb onto the bicycle and pedal furiously

to make the headlight glow. Then a reader would pick up the chapter from the night before. We changed cyclist and reader as often as legs or voice grew tired, working our way through histories, novels, plays.

Father always went upstairs after prayers at 9:15. But the rest of us lingered, reluctant to break the circle, sorry to see the evening end.

8

STORM CLOUDS GATHER

For a year and a half now we had gotten away with our double lives. While we were still an elderly watchmaker living with his two daughters above his tiny shop, the Beje was the center of an underground ring that spread now to the farthest corners of Holland. Here daily came dozens of workers, reports, appeals. Sooner or later we were going to make a mistake.

I especially worried at mealtimes. The dining room was only five steps above street level; a tall passerby could see right in the window. We had hung a white curtain across it providing a kind of screen while letting in light. Still, only when the heavy blackout shades were drawn at night did I feel truly private.

At lunch one day, looking through the thin curtain, I thought I saw a figure standing in the alley. There was no reason for anyone to linger there. I parted the curtain an inch.

Standing there, seemingly immobilized, was old Katrien from Nollie's house!

I bolted down the stairs and pulled her inside. The old lady's hands were cold as ice. "Katrien! What are you doing here?"

"She's gone mad!" she sobbed. "Your sister's gone mad!"

"What happened?"

"They came!" she said. "The S.D.! Your sister and Annaliese were in the living room and I heard her!"

"Heard what?" I nearly screamed.

"They pointed at Annaliese and said, 'Is this a Jew?' Your sister said, 'Yes.'"

I felt my knees go weak. Young, blond Annaliese with the perfect papers. She had trusted us! Oh, Nollie, what had your rigid honesty done?

I left Katrien in the dining room, wheeled my bicycle down the stairs, and bumped as fast as I could the mile and a half to Nollie's street. At the corner, I leaned my bike against a lamp-post and caught my breath. Then, as casually as I was able, I strolled up the sidewalk toward the house. Except for a car parked at the street curb directly in front, everything looked deceptively normal. I walked past. Not a sound from behind the white curtains.

When I got to the corner, I turned around. At that moment the door opened and Nollie came out. Behind her walked a man in a brown business suit. A minute later a second man appeared, half supporting Annaliese. The young woman's face was white as chalk; I thought she would faint. The car doors slammed, the motor roared, and they were gone.

I pedaled back to the Beje fighting tears. Nollie, we soon learned, was taken to the police station to one of the cells in back. But Annaliese had been sent to Amsterdam, from which Jews were transported to concentration camps in Germany and Poland.

It was little Mietje, whose offer of help I had discounted, who kept us in touch with Nollie. She was in wonderful spirits, Mietje said, singing hymns and songs in her sweet soprano. Mietje delivered bread that Betsie baked for Nollie each morning, and the blue sweater Nollie asked for. Mietje relayed another message from Nollie, one especially for me: "No ill will happen to Annaliese. God will not let them take her to Germany. He will not let her suffer because I obeyed Him."

Six days after Nollie's arrest, the telephone rang. Pickwick's voice was on the other end. "I wonder, my dear, if I could trouble you to deliver that watch yourself?"

A message, then, that he could not relay over the phone. I biked at once out to Aerdenhout, taking along a man's watch for safe measure.

Pickwick waited until we were in the drawing room with the door shut. "Last night in Amsterdam, forty Jews were rescued. One of them was most insistent that Nollie know: 'Annaliese is free.' Do you understand this message?"

I nodded, too overcome with relief and joy to speak. How had Nollie been so sure?

After ten days in the Haarlem jail, Nollie was transferred to the prison in Amsterdam. Pickwick said that the German doctor in charge of the prison hospital occasionally arranged a medical discharge. I went at once to Amsterdam to see him. But what could I say, I wondered, as I waited in the entrance hall of his home. How could I get into the good graces of this man?

Lolling about the foyer, sniffing from time to time at my legs and hands, were three huge Doberman pinschers. I remembered the book we were reading aloud by bicycle lamp, *How to Win Friends and Influence People*. One of the techniques advocated was to find the man's hobby. *Hobby, dogs . . . I wonder. . . .*

At last the maid returned and showed me into a small sitting room. "How smart of you, doctor," I said in German to the grizzle-haired man on the sofa, "to have these lovely dogs with you. They must be good company when you must be away from your family."

The doctor's face brightened. "You like dogs?"

For perhaps ten minutes, while I racked my brain for everything I had ever heard or read on the subject, we talked about dogs. Then abruptly the doctor stood up. "But I'm sure you haven't come here to talk about dogs."

I met his eyes. "I have a sister in prison here in Amsterdam. I don't think she's well."

The doctor smiled. "So you aren't interested in dogs."

"I'm interested now," I said, smiling, too. "But I am more interested in my sister."

"What's her name?"

"Nollie van Woerden."

The doctor went out of the room and came back with a brown notebook. "Yes. One of the recent arrivals. Tell me something about her. What is she in prison for?"

Taking a chance, I told the doctor that Nollie's crime had been hiding a Jew. I also told him that she was the mother of six children, who if left without aid could become a burden to the State. (I did not mention that the youngest of these children was now seventeen.)

"Well, we'll see." He walked to the door. "You must excuse me now."

Days, then a week, then two weeks passed and there was no further news. I went back to Amsterdam. "I've come to see how those Dobermans are," I told the doctor.

He was not amused. "I know that you have not come to talk about dogs. You must give me time."

There was nothing to do but wait.

On a bright September noon seventeen of us were squeezed around the dining room table. All of a sudden Nils, one of our workers and seated across from me, turned pale. Nils spoke in a low, normal voice.

"Do not turn around. Someone is looking over the curtain."

But that was impossible. He would have to be ten feet high.

"He's on a ladder, washing the window," Nils said.

Whoever it was, we must not sit here in this frozen, guilty silence! Eusie had an inspiration. "Happy birthday to you!" he sang. We all joined in. "Happy birthday, dear Opa . . . ." The song was still echoing through the Beje when I went out the side door and stood next to the ladder, looking up at the man holding bucket and sponge.

"What are you doing? We didn't want the windows washed. Especially not during the party!"

The man took a piece of paper from his pocket and consulted it. "Isn't this Kuiper's?"

"They're across the street. Please come in and help us

celebrate." The man thanked me, but he had work to do. I watched him cross the Barteljorisstraat with his ladder to Kuiper's.

When I got back to the dining room, they asked, "Do you think he was spying?"

I did not answer. I did not know.

One of my biggest unknowns was my own performance under questioning. As long as I was awake, I felt fairly sure of myself. But if they should come at night . . . Over and over the group worked with me—Nils, Henk, Leendert—bursting into my room without warning, shaking me awake, hurling questions at me.

The first time it happened I was sure the real raid had come. There was a terrific pounding on my door, then the beam of a flashlight in my eyes. "Get up! On your feet!" I could not see the man who was speaking. "Where are you hiding your nine Jews?"

"We only have six Jews now."

There was an awful silence. The room light came on to show Rolf clutching his head with his hands. "Oh, no," he said. "It can't be that bad."

"Think now," said Henk. "The Gestapo is trying to trap you. The answer is, 'What Jews? We don't have Jews here.'"

They tried again a few nights later. "The Jews you're hiding, where do they come from?"

I sat up groggily. "I don't know. They just come to the door."

Rolf flung his hat to the floor. "No, no, no!" he shouted. "'What Jews! There are no Jews!' Can't you learn?"

"I'll learn," I promised. "I'll do better."

And sure enough, the next time I woke a little more completely. Half a dozen shadowy forms filled the room. "Where do you hide the ration cards?" a voice demanded.

Under the bottom stair, of course. But this time I would not be trapped into saying so. A crafty reply occurred to me: "In the Frisian clock on the stairwell!"

Kik sat down beside me and put an arm around me. "That was better, Tante Corrie," he said. "But remember—you *have* no cards except the three for you, Opa, and Tante Betsie."

With repeated drills, I got better. But I worried. When they were real Gestapo agents trained in getting the truth from people, how would I perform?

We were sitting around the supper table after curfew one night, three Ten Booms, the seven "permanent guests," and two Jews for whom we were seeking homes, when the shop doorbell chimed.

Someone bold enough to stand there after curfew? Taking the keys from my pocket, I hurried down to the hall, unlocked the workshop door, and felt my way through the dark store. At the front door I listened a moment.

"Who's there?" I called.

"Do you remember me?" A man speaking German.

"Who is it?" I asked in the same language.

"An old friend. Open the door!"

I fumbled with the lock and drew the door gingerly back. It was a German soldier in uniform. Before I could reach the alarm button behind the door, he had pushed his way inside. He took off his hat, and I recognized the young German watchmaker whom Father had discharged four years ago.

"Otto!" I cried.

"Captain Altschuler," he corrected me.

I said nothing. He looked around the shop.

"Same stuffy little place," he said. He reached for the wall switch, but I put my hand over it.

"No! We don't have blackout shades in the shop!"

"Well, let's go upstairs where we can talk over old times. Your father still alive?"

I edged my way to the sales counter where another bell was located. "Father is well, thank you."

"Aren't you going to invite me up to pay my respects?"

Why was he so eager to go upstairs? My finger found the button.

"What was that?" Otto whirled around.

"What was what?"

"That sound! I heard a kind of buzzing." Otto started back through the workshop.

"Wait!" I shouted. "Let me get the front door locked and I'll go up with you! I want to see how long it takes them to recognize you."

I dawdled at the door as long as I dared; his suspicions were aroused. I followed him into the hall. Not a sound from the dining room or the stairs. I dashed past him up the steps and rapped on the door.

"Father! Betsie!" I cried in what I hoped was a playful voice. "I'll give you three guesses who's standing here!"

"No guessing games!" Otto reached past me and flung open the door.

Father and Betsie looked up from their meal. The table was set for three, my unfinished plate on the other side. It was so

perfect that even I, who had just seen twelve people eating here, could scarcely believe this was anything but an innocent old man dining with his daughters. The Alpina sign stood on the sideboard. They had remembered everything.

Otto pulled out a chair. "Well!" he crowed. "Things happened just like I said, didn't they?"

"So it would seem," said Father mildly.

Otto lingered around fifteen minutes. Then, feeling perhaps that he had underlined his victory sufficiently, he sauntered out into the empty streets.

It was only after another half hour that we dared give the all clear to nine cramped and shaky people.

The second week in October, the secret telephone number rang in the hall. I hurried to pick it up; only Father, Betsie, or I answered it.

"Aren't you coming to pick me up?"

It was Nollie.

"Nollie! Where are you?"

"At the train station in Amsterdam!

"Stay right there!"

I biked to Nollie's house and then with Flip and the children hurried to the Haarlem station. We saw Nollie in Amsterdam in her bright blue sweater even before our train came to a stop.

Seven weeks in prison had left her pale, but as radiantly Nollie as ever. A prison doctor, she said, had pronounced her low blood pressure a serious condition, one that might leave her disabled and her six children a burden to society. Her face wrinkled in puzzlement as she said it.

Christmas of 1943 was approaching.

At the Beje, we had not only Christmas to celebrate but also Hanukkah, the Jewish Festival of Lights. Betsie found a Hanukkah candlestand among the treasures stored with us behind the dining room cupboard and set it on the upright piano. Each night we lit one more candle, and then we would sing.

About the fifth night as we were gathered round the piano, the doorbell in the alley rang. I opened it to find the wife of the optician next door, her plump face twisted with anxiety.

"Do you think," she whispered, "your Jews could sing a little more softly? We can hear them and—well, there are all kinds of people on this street. . . ."

Back in Tante Jans' rooms, we considered this news in consternation. If our neighbors knew about our affairs, how many other people in Haarlem did?

It was not long before we discovered that one was the chief of police himself. One dark January morning, Toos burst into Tante Jans' rear room clutching a letter in her hand. The envelope bore the seal of the Haarlem police.

I tore it open. Inside, on the police chief's

stationery, was a handwritten note. "You will come to my office this afternoon at three o'clock."

For twenty minutes we tried to analyze that note. Some felt it was not a prelude to arrest. Still, it was safest to prepare for search and imprisonment. Workers slipped out of the house, one at a time. Boarders emptied wastebaskets and picked up scraps of sewing in preparation for a quick flight to the secret room. I burned incriminating papers in the coal hearth in the dining room.

Then I took a bath and packed a prison bag according to what Nollie and others had learned: a Bible, a pencil, needle and thread, soap, toothbrush, and comb. I dressed in my warmest clothes with a second sweater beneath the top one. Then I hugged Father and Betsie tight and walked to the police station

The policeman on duty looked at the letter. "This way," he said.

He knocked at the door marked Chief. The man who sat behind the desk had red-gray hair combed over a bald spot. A radio was playing. The chief reached over and twisted the volume knob up.

"Miss ten Boom," he said. "Welcome."

"How do you do, sir."

The chief had left his desk to shut the door behind me. "Do sit down," he said. "I know all about you, you know. About your work."

"The watchmaking you mean."

"No." The chief lowered his voice. "I am talking about another work, and I want you to know that some of us here are in sympathy."

The chief was smiling broadly now. Tentatively I smiled back.

"Now, Miss ten Boom," he went on, "I have a request." He dropped his voice. He was, he said, working with the underground himself. But an informer in the police department was leaking information to the Gestapo. "There's no way for us to deal with this man but to kill him."

A shudder went down my spine.

The chief went on in a whisper. "If he remains at large, many others will die. That is why I wondered, Miss ten Boom, if in your work *you* might know of someone who could—"

"Kill him?"

"Yes."

I leaned back. Was this a trap?

"Sir," I said at last, "I have always believed that it was my role to save life, not destroy it. I understand your dilemma, however, and I have a suggestion. Are you a praying man?"

"Aren't we all, these days?"

"Then let us pray together now that God will reach the heart of this man so that he does not continue to betray his countrymen."

There was a long pause. Then the chief nodded. "That I would very much like to do."

There in the heart of the police station, with the radio blaring out the latest news of the German advance, we prayed. We prayed that this Dutchman would come to realize his worth in the sight of God and the worth of every other human being on earth.

At the end of the prayer, the chief stood up. "Thank you, Miss ten Boom." He shook my hand. "I know now that it was wrong to ask you."

Still clutching my prison bag, I walked home. I did not tell Father and Betsie that we had been asked to kill.

The episode with the chief of police should have been encouraging in that apparently we had friends in high places. But the news had the opposite effect. All of Haarlem seemed to know what we were up to. How could we stop? We had to go on, but we knew that disaster could not be long in coming.

It came first to Jop, the apprentice who had sought a safe home at the Beje.

Late one afternoon near the end of January 1944, Rolf stepped into the workshop. He glanced at Jop. I nodded: Jop was party to everything that went on in the house.

"There's an underground home in Ede that is going to be raided this evening. Do you have anyone who can go?"

I did not.

"I'll go," Jop said.

I opened my mouth to protest that he was inexperienced. Then I thought of the unsuspecting people at Ede. We had a wardrobe of girls' scarves and dresses upstairs. . . .

"Then quickly, boy," Rolf said. "You must leave immediately." He gave Jop the details and hurried away. In a few moments Jop reappeared, making a very pretty brunette in long coat and kerchief. To my astonishment he turned at the door and kissed me.

Jop was supposed to be back by the 7:00 p.m. curfew. Seven came and went. Perhaps he had been delayed and would return in the morning.

Early the next day, I knew the minute Rolf stepped through the door that bad news was weighing him down.

"It's Jop, isn't it?"

"Yes." Rolf learned the story from the sergeant at the night desk. When Jop got to the address in Ede, the Gestapo was already there. Jop had rung the bell; the door opened. Pretending to be the owner of the house, the S.D. man had invited Jop in.

"And, Corrie," Rolf said, "we must face it. The Gestapo will get information out of Jop."

That night Father and Betsie and I prayed long after the others had gone to bed. We knew that in spite of daily mounting risks we had no choice but to move forward. This was evil's hour; we could not run away from it. Perhaps only when human effort had done its best and failed would God's power alone be free to work.

9

THE RAID

It was the morning of February 28, 1944. For two days I had been in bed with influenza. My head throbbed, my joints were on fire, and I drifted in and out of feverish sleep.

Suddenly Betsie was standing at the foot of the bed. "I'm sorry to wake you, Corrie. But there's a man down in the shop who insists he will talk only to you."

"Who is he?"

"I've never seen him before."

I sat up shakily. "That's all right. I have to get up anyway."

I struggled to my feet. There by the bed lay my prison bag, packed and ready as it had been since the summons from the chief of police. Besides the Bible, clothing, and toilet things, it now held vitamins, aspirin, and much else. It had become a kind of safety for me against the terrors of prison.

I got slowly into my clothes and stepped out onto the landing. The house seemed to reel around me. As I crept downstairs, clinging to the handrail, I was surprised to hear voices. I looked into Tante Jans' rooms; I had forgotten people were gathering for Willem's weekly service. Peter was at the piano. I continued down around the stairs, passing new arrivals streaming up.

As I arrived in the shop, a sandy-haired man sprang forward. "Miss ten Boom!"

"Yes?" There was an old Dutch expression: You can tell a man by the way he meets your eyes. This man seemed to concentrate somewhere between my nose and my chin. "Is it about a watch?" I asked.

"No, Miss ten Boom!" His eyes seemed to make a circle around my face. "My wife has been arrested. We've been hiding Jews. If she is questioned, all of our lives are in danger."

"I don't know how *I* can help," I said.

"I need six hundred guilders. There's a policeman at the station who can be bribed for that amount. I'm a poor man—and I've been told you have certain contacts."

"Contacts?"

"Miss ten Boom! It's a matter of life and death! If I don't get it right away, she'll be taken to Amsterdam and then it will be too late."

Something about the man's behavior made me hesitate. And yet how could I risk being wrong? "Come back in half an hour. I'll have the money," I said.

For the first time the man's eyes met mine.

The amount was more than we had at the Beje, so I sent Toos to the bank and struggled back up the stairs. Where earlier I had been burning with fever, now I was shaking with cold. In my room, I undressed, refilled the vaporizer, and climbed back into bed. Soon I was asleep.

In my fevered dream a buzzer kept ringing. On and on it went. Feet were running, voices whispering. "Hurry! Hurry!"

I sat bolt upright. People were running past my bed. I turned in time to see Thea's heels disappear through the low door. Meta was behind her, then Henk. Eusie dashed past me, his pipe rattling in the ashtray that he carried in shaking hands.

At last it penetrated my brain that the emergency had come. I counted the people crawling into the secret room. *But where is Mary?* She appeared in the bedroom door, mouth open, gasping for air. I sprang from my bed and pulled her across the room.

I was sliding the secret panel down behind her when a slim white-haired man burst into the room. I recognized him from Pickwick's, someone high in the national Resistance. I had had no idea he was in the house. He dived after Mary. The man's legs vanished and I dropped the panel down. I pushed my prison bag up against the panel. Below I heard doors slamming, heavy footsteps on the stairs. But it was another sound that turned my blood to water: the rasp of Mary's breathing.

"Lord Jesus!" I prayed. "You have the power to heal! Heal Mary now!"

I had just gotten in bed again when the bedroom door flew open.

"What's your name?"

I sat up slowly.

"What?"

"Your name!"

"Cornelia ten Boom." The man wore an ordinary business suit. He turned and shouted down the stairs, "We've got one more up here, Willemse." He turned back to me. "Get up! Get dressed!"

As I crawled out from under the covers, the man took a slip of paper from his pocket and consulted it. "So you're the ring leader!" He looked at me with new interest. "Where are you hiding the Jews?"

"I don't know what you're talking about."

The man laughed. "And you don't know anything about an underground ring, either. We'll see about that!"

He had not taken his eyes off me, so I began to pull on my clothes over my pajamas, ears straining for a sound from the secret room.

"Let me see your papers!"

I pulled out the little sack that I wore around my neck. The man took my papers and looked at them. For a moment the room was silent. Mary Itallie's wheeze—why wasn't I hearing it?

The man threw the papers back at me. "Hurry up!"

He was not in half the hurry I was to get away from that room. I buttoned my sweater wrong in my haste and stuffed my feet into my shoes without bothering to tie them.

I was about to reach for my prison bag. It stood where I had shoved it in my panic: directly in front of the secret

panel. I could not reach down under the shelf to get it, not with this man watching my every move.

It was the hardest thing I had ever done to walk out of that room, leaving the bag behind.

I stumbled down the stairs, my knees shaking. A soldier was stationed in front of Tante Jans' rooms; the door was shut. I wondered if the prayer meeting had ended, if Willem and Nollie and Peter had gotten away. Or were they all still in there? How many innocent people might be involved?

The man behind me gave me a little push, and I hurried on down the stairs to the dining room. Father, Betsie, and Toos were sitting on chairs pulled back against the wall. Beside them sat three underground workers who must have arrived since I had gone upstairs. On the floor beneath the window, broken in three pieces, lay the Alpina sign. Someone had managed to knock it from the sill.

A second Gestapo agent in plain clothes was pawing through a pile of silver and jewelry heaped on the dining room table. The space behind the corner cupboard had been indeed the first place they looked.

"Here's the other one," said the man who had brought me down. "My information says she's the leader of the whole outfit."

The man at the table, the one called Willemse, glanced at me, then turned back to the loot in front of him. "You know what to do, Kapteyn."

Kapteyn seized me by the elbow and shoved me ahead of him down the remaining five steps and into the rear of the shop. Another soldier in uniform stood guard inside this door. Kapteyn prodded me through to the front room and pushed me against the wall.

"Where are the Jews?"

"There aren't any Jews here."

The man struck me hard across the face.

"Where do you hide the ration cards?"

"I don't know what you're—"

Kapteyn hit me again. I staggered up against the wall. Before I could recover he slapped me again, then again, and again, stinging blows that jerked my head backward.

"Where are the Jews?"

Another blow.

"Where is your secret room?"

I tasted blood in my mouth. My head spun, my ears rang. "Lord Jesus," I cried out, "protect me!"

Kapteyn's hand stopped in midair. His arm slowly dropped to his side. "If you won't talk, that skinny one will."

I stumbled ahead of him back up the stairs. He pushed me into one of the chairs against the dining room wall. Through a blur, I saw him lead Betsie from the room.

Above us hammer blows and splintering wood showed where a squad of trained searchers was probing for the secret room. Then down in the alley the doorbell rang. But did they not see the Alpina sign was gone . . . ? I glanced at the window. There on the sill, the broken pieces fitted carefully together, sat the wooden triangle.

I looked up to see Willemse staring at me. "I thought so!" he said. "It was a signal!"

He ran down the stairs. I heard the alley door open and Willemse's smooth voice. "Come in, won't you?"

"Have you heard!" A woman's voice. "They've got Oom Herman!"

Not Pickwick!

"Oh?" I heard Willemse say. "Who was with him?" He pumped her for information, then placed her under arrest. Blinking with fright, the woman was seated with us along the wall. I recognized her only as a person who occasionally took messages for us about the city. I stared in anguish at the sign in the window announcing to the world that all was as usual at the Beje. Our home had been turned into a trap. How many more would fall into it before this day was over?

Kapteyn appeared with Betsie in the dining room door. Her lips were swollen and puffy, a bruise darkening on her cheek. She half fell into the chair next to mine.

Two men were clumping down the stairs carrying something. They had discovered the old radio beneath the stairs.

"Law-abiding citizens, are you?" Kapteyn went on. "You! Old man there. I see you believe in the Bible." He jerked his thumb at the well-worn book on its shelf. "What does it say in there about obeying the government?"

"'Fear God,'" Father quoted, and on his lips the words came as blessing and reassurance. "'Fear God and honor the queen.'"

Kapteyn stared at him. "The Bible doesn't say that."

"No," Father admitted. "It says, 'Fear God and honor the king.' In our case, that is the queen."

"We're the government now," roared Kapteyn, "and you're all lawbreakers!"

The doorbell rang. Again there were questions and an arrest. It seemed to me that we had never had so many callers. At least, from the banging and thumping above, they had not discovered the secret room.

A new sound made me jump. The phone down in the hall was ringing.

Willemse grabbed me by the wrist and yanked me down the stairs behind him. He thrust the receiver up against my ear but kept his hand on it.

"Answer!" he hissed.

"This is the Ten Boom residence and shop," I said stiffly.

The person on the other end did not catch the strangeness in my voice. "Miss ten Boom, you're in terrible danger! They've arrested Herman Sluring! They know everything!" On and on she babbled, the man at my side hearing everything.

She had scarcely hung up when the phone rang again. A man's voice, and again the message, "Oom Herman's been taken to the police station. That means they're on to everything. . . ."

At last, the third time I repeated my formal and not typical greeting, there was a click on the other end and the line went dead. Willemse shoved me back up the stairs and into my chair. "Our friends wised up," he told Kapteyn. "But I heard enough."

A man appeared in the doorway. "We've searched the whole place, Willemse," he said. "If there's a secret room here, the devil himself built it."

Willemse looked from Betsie to Father to me. "There's a secret room," he said. "And people are using it. We'll set a guard around the house till they've turned to mummies."

It had been half an hour since the doorbell had rung last. Word was out: no one else would walk into the trap at the Beje. Apparently Willemse had come to the same conclusion because abruptly he ordered us on our feet and down to the hallway with our coats and hats. Father, Betsie, and me he held in the dining room till last.

In front of us down the stairs came the people from Tante Jans' rooms. I held my breath scanning them. Apparently most of those at the prayer service had left before the raid. But here came Nollie, Peter, and Willem. The whole family. Father, all four of his children, one grandchild.

Kapteyn gave me a shove. "Get moving."

Father took his hat from the wall peg. Outside the dining room door, he paused to pull up the weights on the old Frisian clock.

"We mustn't let the clock run down," he said.

Father! Do you really think we will be back home when next the chain runs out?

We marched through the alley and into the Smedestraat. By the time we got inside the police station, I was shaking with cold. We were herded along a corridor and into a large room that had been a gymnasium. A desk stood in the center with a German army officer seated behind it. Tumbling mats had been spread out to cover part of the floor, and I collapsed onto one of them.

For two hours the officer took down names, addresses, and other statistics. I counted 35 people who were arrested from the raid on the Beje.

People from previous arrests were sitting or lying about on the mats, too, some of them faces we knew. I looked for Pickwick, but he was not among them.

At last the officer left. For the first time since the alarm buzzer sounded, we could talk among ourselves. I soon fell into a fitful sleep, but was waked by the heavy door of the gym slamming open. In strode Rolf.

"Let's have it quiet in here!" he shouted. "Toilets are out back," he continued in a loud voice. "You can go one at a time under escort."

Beside the row of outdoor toilets was a basin with a tin cup on a chain. Gratefully I took a long drink—the first since morning. Toward evening a policeman carried into the gym a large basket of fresh hot rolls. I could not swallow mine.

In the evening, a group gathered around Father for prayers. Every day of my life had ended like this: that deep steady voice, entrusting us all to the care of God. His blue eyes seemed to be seeing beyond the locked and crowded room, beyond Haarlem, beyond earth itself, as he quoted from memory: "Thou art my hiding place and my shield: I hope in thy word. . . . Hold thou me up, and I shall be safe. . . ."

None of us slept much. In the morning, the police again brought rolls. I dozed with my back up against the wall; the worst pain now seemed to be in my chest. It was noon when soldiers entered the room and ordered us on our feet. We struggled into our coats and filed again through the cold corridors.

In the Smedestraat a wall of people pressed against police barricades set across the street. As Betsie and I stepped out with Father between us, a murmur of horror greeted the sight of "Haarlem's Grand Old Man" being led to prison. In front of the door stood a bus with soldiers occupying the rear seats. People climbed aboard while friends and relatives in the crowd wept or simply stared. Betsie and I gripped Father's arms to start down the steps. Then we froze. Stumbling past us between two soldiers, hatless and coatless, came Pickwick. The top of his bald head was a welter of bruises. He did not look up as he was hauled onto the bus.

Father, Betsie, and I squeezed into a double seat near the front. Through the window I caught a glimpse of Tine standing in the crowd. The bus shuddered and started up. Police cleared a path and we inched forward. I gazed out the window, holding onto Haarlem with my eyes. Now we were crossing the Grote Markt. . . .

Then I recalled.

The vision. I had seen it all. Willem, Nollie, Pickwick, Peter—all of us here—drawn against our wills across this square. It had been in the dream—all of us leaving Haarlem, unable to turn back. Going where?

10

SCHEVENINGEN

A two-hour drive brought us into the streets of The Hague. The bus stopped in front of a new building; word was whispered back that this was Gestapo headquarters for all of Holland. We were marched into a large room, where the endless process of taking down names, addresses, and occupations began all over again.

The chief interrogator's eye fell on Father. "That old man!" he cried. "Did he have to be arrested?"

Willem led Father up to the desk. The Gestapo chief leaned forward. "I'd like to send you home, old fellow," he said. "I'll take your word that you won't cause any more trouble."

I could not see Father's face, but I heard his answer.

"If I go home today," he said evenly and clearly, "tomorrow I will open my door again to anyone in need."

The amiability drained from the other man's face. "Get back in line!" he shouted.

As we inched along the counter, there were endless repetitions of questions, endless consulting of papers, endless coming and going of officials. It was night when we were marched at last out of the building. We made out the bulk of a large canvas-roofed army truck. Two soldiers had to lift Father over the tailgate. There was no sign of Pickwick. Father, Betsie, and I found places to sit on a narrow bench that ran around the sides.

The truck had no springs and bounced roughly over the bomb-pitted streets of The Hague. I slipped my arm behind Father's back to keep him from striking the edge. Willem, standing near the back, whispered out what he could see of the blacked-out city. We left the downtown section and seemed to be headed toward the suburb of Scheveningen. It appeared now that our destination was the federal penitentiary.

The truck jerked to a halt, and behind us massive gates clanged shut. We entered an enormous courtyard surrounded by a high brick wall. The truck backed up to a long low building; soldiers prodded us inside. I blinked in the white glare of bright ceiling lights. I felt a shove from behind and found myself staring at cracked plaster. I turned my eyes as far as I could, first left and then right. There was Willem. Two places away from him, Betsie. Next to me on the other side was Toos. All like me, standing with their faces to the wall. Where was Father?

Then somewhere to the right a door opened.

"Women prisoners follow me!"

As I stepped away from the wall, I glanced swiftly around the room for Father. There he was—a few feet from the wall, seated in a straight-backed chair one of the guards had brought him.

We started down the long corridor that I could see through the door. But I hung back, gazing desperately at Father, Willem, Peter, all our brave underground workers.

"Father!" I cried. "God be with you!"

His head turned toward me. The overhead light flashed from his glasses.

"And with you, my daughters," he said.

I turned and followed the others. Behind me the door slammed closed. *Oh, Father, when will I see you next?*

Betsie's hand slipped around mine

Ahead of us in the corridor was a desk, behind it a woman in uniform. As each prisoner reached this point, she gave her name for the thousandth time that day and placed on the desk whatever she was wearing of value. Nollie, Betsie, and I unstrapped our beautiful wristwatches. The officer pointed to the simple gold ring that had belonged to Mama. I wriggled it from my finger and laid it on the desk.

The procession down the corridor continued. The walls on both sides of us were lined with narrow metal doors. Now the column of women halted; the matron was fitting a key into one of the doors. The door banged shut; the column moved on. Another door unlocked, another human being closed behind it. No two from Haarlem in the same cell.

Betsie stepped through a door first; before she could turn or say good-bye, it had closed. Two cells farther on, Nollie left me.

Now the corridor branched and we turned left. Then right, then left again, an endless world of steel and concrete.

"Ten Boom, Cornelia."

Another door rasped open. The cell was deep and narrow, scarcely wider than the door. A woman lay on the single cot, three others on straw ticks on the floor. "Give this one the cot," the matron said. "She's sick."

A spasm of coughing seized my chest and throat.

"We don't want a sick woman in here!" someone shouted. They were stumbling to their feet, backing away from me.

"I'm so sorry—" I began, but another voice interrupted me. "It isn't your fault. Come on, Frau Mikes, give her the cot." The young woman turned to me. "Let me hang up your hat and coat."

Gratefully I handed her my hat, which she added to a row of clothes hanging from hooks along one wall. I kept my coat wrapped tight around me. The cot had been vacated, and I moved shakily toward it, trying not to sneeze or breathe. I sank down on the narrow bed, then went into fresh coughing as a cloud of dust rose from the filthy straw mattress. At last the attack passed and I lay down. The sour straw smell filled my nostrils.

I will never be able to sleep on such a bed, I thought, and the next thing I knew it was morning and there was a clattering at the door. "Food call," my cellmates told me. I struggled to my feet. A square of metal had dropped open in the door, forming a small shelf. Onto this someone in the hall was placing tin plates filled with a steaming gruel.

"There's a new one here!" Frau Mikes called out. "We get five portions!" Another tin plate was slammed onto the shelf.

I picked up my plate, stared at the watery gray porridge, and handed it silently to Frau Mikes to eat. In a little while the plates were collected and the pass-through in the door slammed shut.

Later in the morning a key grated in the lock, the bolt banged, and the door opened long enough for the sanitary bucket to be passed out. The wash basin was also emptied and returned with clean water. The women picked up their straw pallets from the floor and piled them in a corner, raising a fresh storm of dust that started me coughing again.

Then a prison boredom—which I soon learned to fear above all else—settled over the cell. At first I attempted to relieve it by talking with the others, but though they were as courteous as people can be who are living literally on top of one another, they turned aside my questions. I eventually realized that prisoners instinctively shied away from questions about their larger lives.

For the first days of imprisonment, I stayed in a frenzy of anxiety about Father, Betsie, Willem, Pickwick. But these thoughts led to such despair that I learned not to give in to them.

I was finding it hard to sit up. Increasingly I was spending the days as I did the nights, tossing on the thin straw pallet trying in vain to find a position in which my aches were eased. My head throbbed continually, pain shot up and down my arms, my cough brought up blood.

I was thrashing feverishly on the cot one morning when the cell door opened and there stood a steel-voiced matron.

"Ten Boom, Cornelia."

I struggled to my feet.

"Come with me."

My coat I was wearing already, but I took my hat from its hook and stepped out into the corridor. The matron relocked the door, then set off so rapidly that my heart hammered as I trotted after her. At last we stepped out into the broad, high-walled courtyard. For the first time in two weeks, blue sky! How high the clouds were, how white and clean.

"Quick!" snapped the matron.

I hurried to a shiny black automobile. She opened the rear door and I got in. Two others were already in the backseat, a soldier and a woman with a gray face. Next to the driver slumped a desperately ill–looking man. As the car started up, the woman beside me lifted a blood-stained towel to her mouth and coughed into it. I understood: The three of us were ill.

The massive prison gate opened and we were in the outside world, spinning along broad city streets. I stared in wonderment through the window. People walking, looking in store windows, talking with friends. Had I been as free as that only two weeks ago?

The car parked before an office building. We entered a waiting room jammed with people and sat down under the watchful eyes of the soldier. When nearly an hour had passed, I asked permission to use the lavatory. The soldier spoke to the trim white-uniformed nurse behind the reception desk.

"This way," she said crisply. She took me down a short hall, stepped into the bathroom with me, and shut the door. "Quick! Is there any way I can help?"

I blinked at her. "Oh, yes! Could you get me a Bible? And a needle and thread! A toothbrush! And soap!"

She bit her lip doubtfully. "I'll do what I can." And she was gone.

But her kindness shone in the little room as brightly as the gleaming white tiles and shiny faucets. My heart soared as I scrubbed the grime off my neck and face.

A man's voice at the door: "Come on! You've been in there long enough!"

I rinsed off the soap and followed the soldier back to the waiting room. The nurse did not look up. After another long wait my name was called. The doctor asked me to cough, took my temperature and blood pressure, applied his stethoscope, and announced that I had pleurisy.

He wrote something on a sheet of paper. Then he laid a hand for an instant on my shoulder. "I hope," he said in a low voice, "that I am doing you a favor with this diagnosis."

In the waiting room the soldier was on his feet ready for me. As I crossed the room, the nurse rose briskly from her desk and swished past me. In my hand I felt a small something wrapped in paper.

I slid it into my coat pocket as I followed the soldier down the stairs. The other woman was already back in the car; the sick man did not reappear. All during the return ride my hand strayed to the object in my pocket.

The high walls loomed ahead, and then the gate rang shut behind us. At last, at the end of the long echoing corridors, I reached my cell. My cellmates crowded around me as I un-wrapped the package from my pocket.

Two bars of pre-war soap appeared. No toothbrush or needle, but a whole packet of safety pins! Most wonderful of all, in four small booklets, the four gospels.

I shared the soap and pins among the five of us. But though I offered to divide the books as well, they refused. I stretched my aching body on the foul straw and clutched the precious books between my hands.

Two evenings later the cell door banged open and a guard strode in.

"Ten Boom, Cornelia," she snapped. "Get your things."

I said farewell to the others with my eyes and followed the woman into the hall. She paused to lock the door, then marched

off down the corridor, heading deeper into the maze of prison passageways.

She halted in front of a door and opened it with a key. I stepped inside. The door clanged behind me. The bolt slammed shut.

The cell was identical to the one I had just left, six steps long, two wide, a single cot at the back. But this one was empty. As the guard's footsteps died away down the corridor, I leaned against the cold metal of the door. *Alone.*

I must not let my thoughts run wildly. Sit down on the cot. This one reeked even worse than the other. I reached for the blanket. Someone had been sick on it. I thrust it away, but it was too late. I dashed for the bucket near the door and leaned weakly over it.

At that moment the lightbulb in the ceiling went out. I groped back to the cot and huddled there in the dark, setting my teeth against the stink of the bedding, wrapping my coat tighter about me. The cell was bitter cold. What had I done to be separated from people this way?

In the morning my fever was worse. I could not stand even long enough to get my food from the shelf in the door, and after an hour or so the plate was taken away untouched.

Toward evening the pass-through dropped open again and the hunk of coarse prison bread appeared. By now I was desperate for food but less able to walk than ever. Whoever was in the hall must have seen the problem. A hand picked up the bread and hurled it toward me. It landed on the floor beside the cot. I clawed for it and gnawed it greedily.

For several days while the fever raged, my supper was delivered in this manner. Mornings the door squealed open and a woman carried the plate of hot gruel to the cot. I was as starved for the sight of a human face as for the food and tried in a hoarse croak to start a conversation. But the woman, obviously a fellow prisoner, would only shake her head with a fearful glance toward the hall.

The door also opened once a day to let in the trustee from Medical Supply with a dose of some yellow liquid from a very dirty bottle.

This same trustee was also charged with recording my temperature each time. By the end of the week, an irritable voice called through the food slot, "Get up and get the food yourself! Your fever's gone—you won't be waited on again!"

I felt sure that the fever had not gone, but I would creep, trembling, to the door for my plate. When I had replaced it I would lie down again on the smelly straw.

Thoughts, now that I was alone, were a bigger problem than ever. I could not pray for family and friends by name, so great was the fear and longing wrapped around each one. "Those I love, Lord," I would say. "You know them. You see them. Oh—bless them all!"

Thoughts were enemies. That prison bag . . . how many times I opened it in my mind and pawed through all the things I had left behind. *A blouse. Aspirin, a whole bottle of them. Toothpaste with a pepperminty taste, and—*

Then I would catch myself. If I had it to do again, would I put these little personal comforts ahead of human lives? Of course not. But in the dark cold nights, as the fever pulsed, I would draw that bag out of some dark corner of my mind and root through it once again. *A towel to lay on this scratchy straw. An aspirin . . .*

This cell had a window. Seven iron bars ran across it, four bars up and down. It was much too high to look out of, but I could see the sky.

All day I kept my eyes fixed on that bit of heaven. Sometimes clouds moved across the squares, white or pink or edged with gold, and when the wind was from the west I could hear the sea. Best of all, for nearly an hour each day, gradually lengthening as the spring sun rose higher, a shaft of checkered light streamed into the dark little room. As the weather turned warm and I grew stronger, I would stand up to catch the sunshine on my face and chest, moving along the wall with the moving light, climbing at last onto the cot to stand on tiptoe in the final rays.

As my health returned, I read the gospels, seeing whole the magnificent drama of salvation. And as I did, an incredible thought prickled the back of my neck. Was it possible that this war, Scheveningen prison, this very cell, none of it was unforeseen or accidental? Could it be part of the pattern first revealed in the gospels? Had not Jesus—and here my reading became intent indeed—been defeated as utterly as our little group and our small plans had been?

But . . . if the gospels were truly the pattern of God's activity, then defeat was only the beginning. I would look around at the bare little cell and wonder what conceivable victory could come from a place like this.

A woman in the first cell had taught me to make a kind of knife by rubbing a corset stay against the rough cement floor. It seemed to me important not to lose track of time. So with a sharp-honed stay, I scratched a calendar on the wall behind the cot. As each long day crawled to a close, I checked off another square. I also started a record of special dates beneath the calendar:

February 28, 1944   Arrest
February 29, 1944   Transport to Scheveningen
March 16, 1944   Beginning of Solitary

And now a new date:

April 15, 1944   My Birthday in Prison

Two days after my birthday I was taken for the first time to the shower room. A grim-faced guard marched beside me, but nothing could dim the wonder of stepping into that wide corridor after so many weeks of close confinement.

At the door to the shower room, several women were waiting. Even in the strict silence this human closeness was joy and strength. I scanned the faces of those coming out, but neither Betsie nor Nollie was there, nor anyone else from Haarlem.

The shower was glorious—warm, clean water over my festering skin, streams of water through my matted hair. I went back to my cell with a new resolve: The next time I was permitted a shower, I would take with me three of my gospels. Solitary was teaching me that it was not possible to be rich alone.

I was not alone much longer. Into my solitary cell came a small, busy black ant. I had almost put my foot where he was one morning when I realized the honor being done me. I crouched down and admired the marvelous design of legs and body. I promised I would not so thoughtlessly stride about again.

After a while he disappeared through a crack in the floor. But when my evening piece of bread appeared on the door shelf, I scattered some crumbs, and to my joy he popped out almost at once. He picked up a piece, struggled down the hole with it, and came back for more. It was the beginning of a relationship.

Now, in addition to the daily visit of the sun, I had the company of this brave and handsome guest—soon of a whole small committee. If I was washing out clothes in the basin or sharpening the point on my homemade knife when the ants appeared, I stopped at once to give them my full attention. It would have been unthinkable to squander two activities on the same bit of time!

One evening I heard shouts far down the corridor. They were answered closer by. Now noisy voices came from every direction. How unusual for the prisoners to be making a racket! Where were the guards?

The shelf in my door had not been closed since the bread came two hours ago. I pressed my ear to it and listened, but it was hard to make sense of the tumult outside. The guards must all be away!

"Please!" a voice pleaded. "Let's use this time before they get back!"

"What's happening?" I cried through the open slot. "Where are the guards?"

"At the party," the same voice answered me. "It's Hitler's birthday."

People shouted their names down the corridor. This was our chance to tell where we were, to get information.

"I'm Corrie ten Boom!" I called through the food shelf. "My whole family is here somewhere! Has anyone seen Casper ten Boom? Betsie ten Boom! Nollie van Woerden! Willem ten Boom!" I shouted names until I was hoarse and heard them repeated from mouth to mouth down the long corridor. I passed names, too, to the right and left, as we worked out a kind of system.

After a while answers began to filter back. Along with personal messages were rumors about the world outside. At last some of the names I had shouted out began to return. "Betsie ten Boom is in cell 312. She says to tell you that God is good."

Oh, that was every inch Betsie!

Then: "Nollie van Woerden was released more than a month ago." Released! Oh, thank God!

Toos, too, released!

News from the mens' section was longer returning, but as it did my heart leaped higher and higher:

Peter van Woerden. Released!

Herman Sluring. Released!

Willem ten Boom. Released!

As far as I could discover, every single one taken in the raid on the Beje—with the exception of Betsie and me—had been freed. Only about Father could I discover no news at all, although I called his name over and over into the murmuring hall. No one seemed to have seen him. No one seemed to know.

It was perhaps a week later that my cell door opened and a prison trustee tossed a package wrapped in brown paper onto the floor. I picked it up, hefted it, turned it over and over. The wrapping paper had been torn open and carelessly retied, but even through the disarray I could spot Nollie's loving touch. I sat on the cot and opened it.

There, familiar and welcoming as a visit from home, was her light blue sweater. As I put it on, I seemed to feel Nollie's arms circling my shoulders. Also inside the package were cookies and vitamins, needle and thread, and a bright red towel. How Nollie understood the gray color-hunger of prison! She had even wrapped the cookies in red cellophane.

My eyes fell on the postage stamp. Hadn't a message once come to the Beje under a stamp, penciled in the tiny square beneath? I moistened the paper in the basin water and worked the stamp gently free.

There was definitely writing there—but so tiny I had to climb again onto the cot and hold the paper close to the bulb.

"All the watches in your closet are safe."

Safe. Then they had gotten out of the secret room! They had escaped! They were free! How had they managed it? How had they got past the soldiers? *Never mind, dear Lord. You were there, and that is all that matters.*

The cell door opened to let in a German officer followed by the head matron herself. My eyes ran hungrily over the well-pressed uniform with its rows of brilliant colored battle ribbons.

"Miss ten Boom," the officer began in excellent Dutch, "I have a few questions I believe you can help me with."

The matron was carrying a small stool that she set down for the officer. The officer sat down, motioning me to take the cot. He took out a small notebook and began to read names from it.

To my relief I honestly did not know any of the names he read—now I understood the wisdom of the name Mr. Smit. The officer stood up. "Will you be feeling well enough to come for your hearing soon?"

"Yes ... I ... I hope so." The officer stepped out into the hall, the matron scurrying after him with the stool.

On the third of May, I was sitting on my cot sewing. Since Nollie's package had arrived, I had a wonderful new occupation: one by one I was pulling the threads from the red towel and with them embroidering bright figures on the pajamas that I had only recently stopped wearing beneath my clothes. Suddenly the food shelf in the door banged open and shut with a single motion.

There on the floor lay a letter from home—the very first one!

I unfolded the paper. "Corrie, can you be very brave?" I forced my eyes to read on. "I have news that is very hard to write you. Father survived his arrest by only ten days. He is now with the Lord. . . ."

I stood with the paper between my hands so long that the daily shaft of sunlight entered the cell and fell upon it. *Father* . . . The letter glittered in the light as I read the rest. Nollie had no details, not how or where he had died, not even where he was buried.

"Dear Jesus," I finally whispered, "to think that Father sees You now, face to face! To think that he and Mama are together again . . ."

I pulled the cot from the wall and below the calendar scratched another date:

March 9, 1944   Father Released

THE LIEUTENANT

I was walking with a guard down a corridor on a morning in late May. After three months in prison, I had been called for my first hearing.

Lord Jesus, You were called to a hearing, too. Show me what to do.

We stepped into a small interior courtyard. The guard halted in front of a hut and rapped on the door.

"*Ja!*" called a man's voice.

The guard pushed open the door, gave a straight-armed salute, and marched off. The man wore a gun in a leather holster and a beribboned uniform. He was the gentle-mannered man who had visited me in my cell.

"I am Lieutenant Rahms," he said, stepping to the door to close it behind me. "Let me get a fire going."

He filled a potbellied stove with coal. What if this were all a subtle trap? This kind manner—perhaps he had simply found it more effective than brutality in tricking the truth from affection-starved people. *Oh, Lord, let no weak gullibility on my part endanger another's life.*

"I hope," the officer was saying, "we won't have many more days this spring as cold as this one." He drew out a chair for me to sit on.

Warily I accepted it. How strange after three months to feel a chair back behind me, chair arms for my hands! The heat from the stove was quickly warming the little room. In spite of myself, I began to relax. I ventured a timid comment about spring flowers. We talked about flowers for a while, and then he said, "I would like to help you, Miss ten Boom. But you must tell me everything. I may be able to do something, but only if you do not hide anything from me."

For an hour he questioned me, using every psychological trick that the young men of our group had drilled me in. In fact, I felt like a student who has crammed for a difficult exam and then is tested on only the most elementary material.

It soon became clear that they believed the Beje had been a headquarters for raids on food ration offices around the country. Of all the illegal activities I had on my conscience, this was probably the one I knew least about. Other than receiving the stolen cards each month and passing them on, I knew no details of the operation. Apparently my real ignorance began to show; after a while Lieutenant Rahms stopped making notes of my answers.

"Your other activities, Miss ten Boom. What would you like to tell me about them?"

"Other activities? Oh, you mean—you want to know about my church for mentally impaired people!" This was something I had done before the war, and I plunged into an eager account of my efforts at preaching to those with mental challenges.

The lieutenant's eyebrows rose. "What a waste of time and energy!" he exploded at last. "If you want converts, surely one normal person is worth all the half-wits in the world!"

I stared into the man's intelligent eyes. Then to my astonishment I heard my own voice saying boldly, "May I tell you the truth, Lieutenant Rahms?"

"This hearing, Miss ten Boom, is based on the assumption that you will do me that honor."

"The truth, sir," I said, swallowing, "is that God's viewpoint is sometimes different from ours—so different that we could not even guess at it unless He had given us a Book that tells us such things."

I knew it was madness to talk this way to a Nazi officer. But he said nothing, so I plunged ahead. "In the Bible I learned that God values us not for our strength or our brains but simply because He has made us. Who knows, in His eyes a 'half-wit' may be worth more than a watchmaker. Or . . . a lieutenant."

Lieutenant Rahms stood abruptly. "That will be all for today." He walked swiftly to the door. "Guard! The prisoner will return to her cell."

Following the guard through the long cold corridors, I knew I had said too much. I had ruined whatever chance I had that this man might take an interest in my case.

And yet the following morning it was Lieutenant Rahms himself who unlocked my cell door and escorted me to the hearing. In the courtyard this time, a bright sun was shining. "Today," he said, "we will stay outside. You are not getting enough sun."

Gratefully I followed him to the farthest corner of the little yard where the air was warm. We settled our backs against the wall. "I could not sleep last night," the lieutenant said, "thinking about that Book where you have read such different ideas. What else does it say in there?"

On my closed eyelids the sun glimmered and blazed. "It says," I began slowly, "that a Light has come into this world, so that we need no longer walk in the dark. Is there darkness in your life, Lieutenant?"

There was a very long silence.

"There is great darkness," he said at last. "I cannot bear the work I do here."

Then all at once he was telling me about his wife and children, about their garden, their dogs, their summer hiking vacations. "Our town was bombed again last week. Each morning I ask myself, are they still alive?"

"There is One who has them always in His sight, Lieutenant Rahms. Jesus is the Light the Bible shows to me, the Light that can shine even in such darkness as yours."

The man pulled the visor of his hat lower over his eyes; the skull-and-crossbones glinted in the sunlight. When he spoke, it was so low I could hardly hear. "What can you know of darkness like mine . . . ?"

Two more mornings the hearings continued. He had dropped all pretense of questioning me on my underground activities and seemed especially to enjoy hearing about my childhood. Mama, Father, the aunts—he wanted to hear stories about them again and again. He was incensed to learn that Father had died right here in Scheveningen; the documents on my case made no mention of it.

These documents did answer one question: the reason for solitary confinement. "Prisoner's condition contagious to others in cell." I stared at the brief typed words where Lieutenant Rahms' finger rested. I thought of the long nights, the scowling guards, the rule of silence. "But I'm not contagious now! I've been better for weeks, and my own sister is so close! Lieutenant Rahms, if I could only see Betsie! If I could just talk with her a few minutes!"

He lifted his eyes from the desk, and I saw anguish in them. "Miss ten Boom, it is possible that I appear to you as a powerful person. I wear a uniform; I have a certain authority over those under me. But I am in prison, dear lady from Haarlem, a prison stronger than this one."

It was the fourth and final hearing, and we had come back into the small hut for signing the transcript of our meetings. He gathered up the completed paperwork and went out with it, leaving me alone. I was sorry to say good-bye to this man who was struggling so earnestly for truth.

But the lieutenant returned to the room with a guard from the women's wing. "Prisoner ten Boom has completed her hearings," he said, "and will return to her cell."

The young woman snapped to attention. As I stepped through the door, Lieutenant Rahms leaned forward.

"Walk slowly," he said, "in Corridor F."

Walk slowly? What did he mean? The guard strode down the long door-lined halls so swiftly I had to trot to keep up with her. Ahead of us a trustee was unlocking the door of a cell. I trailed behind the guard as much as I dared, my heart thumping wildly. It would be Betsie's cell—I knew it!

Then I was abreast of the door. Betsie's back was to the corridor. I could see only the graceful upswept bun of her hair. The other women in the cell stared curiously into the corridor; her head remained bent over something in her lap. But I had seen the home Betsie had made in Scheveningen.

Unbelievably, against all logic, this cell was charming. My eyes seized details as I inched past. The straw pallets were rolled instead of piled in a heap, standing like little pillars along the walls, each with a lady's hat atop it. A headscarf had somehow been hung along the wall. The contents of several food packages were arranged on a small shelf. Even the coats hanging on their hooks were part of the welcome of that room, each sleeve draped over the shoulder of the coat next to it like a row of dancing children—

I hurried after my escort. It had been a glimpse only, two seconds at the most, but I walked through the corridors of Scheveningen with Betsie's spirit at my side.

All morning I heard doors opening and closing. Now keys rattled outside my own, and a young guard bounded in.

"Prisoner, stand at attention!" she squeaked. I stared at her eyes; the girl was in mortal fear of something or someone.

Then a shadow filled the doorway and the tallest woman I had ever seen stepped into the cell. Her features were classically handsome, and she had the face and height of a goddess—but not a flicker of feeling registered in her eyes.

"No sheets here either, I see," she said in German to the guard. "See that she has two by Friday. One to be changed every two weeks."

The ice-cold eyes appraised me exactly as they had the bed. "How many showers does the prisoner get?"

The guard wet her lips. "About one a week."

One shower a month was closer!

"She will go twice a week."

Sheets! Regular showers! Were conditions going to be better? The new head matron took two strides into the cell; she pointed to a box of soda crackers that had come in a second package from Nollie.

"No boxes in the cells!" cried the little guard in Dutch.

Not knowing what else to do, I dumped the crackers out onto the cot. At the matron's unspoken command, I emptied a bottle of vitamins and a sack of peppermint drops the same way.

Unlike the former head matron, who shrieked and scolded endlessly, this woman worked in a terrifying silence. With a gesture, she directed the guard to feel beneath the mattress. My heart wedged in my throat; my remaining gospel was hidden there. The guard knelt and ran her hands the length of the cot. But whether she was too nervous to do a thorough job or whether there was a more mysterious explanation, she straightened up empty-handed.

And then they were gone.

It was this tall, ramrod-straight woman who unlocked the door to my cell one afternoon in the second half of June and admitted Lieutenant Rahms. At the severity in his face, I swallowed the greeting that had almost burst from me.

"You will come to my office," he said briefly. "The notary has come."

"Notary?" I said.

"For the reading of your Father's will." He made an impatient gesture. "It's the law—family present when a will is opened."

Already he was heading from the cell and down the corridor. I broke into a clumsy run to keep up with the strides of the silent woman beside me. *The law? What law? And since when had the German occupation government concerned itself with Dutch legal procedures? Family present . . . No, don't let yourself think of it!*

At the door to the courtyard the matron turned back along the corridor. I followed Lieutenant Rahms into the dazzling early summer afternoon. He opened the door for me into the hut. Before my eyes adjusted to the gloom, I was drowning in Willem's embrace.

"Corrie! Baby sister!" It was fifty years since he had called me that.

Now Nollie's arm was around me, too, the other one still clinging to Betsie, as though by the strength of her grip she would hold us together forever. Betsie! Nollie! Willem! I did not know which name to cry first. Tine was in that little room, too—and Flip! And another man; when I had time to look, I recognized the Haarlem notary who had been called in on the watch shop's few legal consultations.

We held each other at arm's length to look, and we babbled questions all at once. Betsie was thin and prison-pale. But it was Willem who shocked me. His face was gaunt, yellow, and pain-haunted. He had come home from Scheveningen looking this way, Tine told me. Two of the eight men crowded into his tiny cell had died while he was there.

I could not bear to see him this way. I crooked my arm through his, standing close so that I did not have to look at him, loving the sound of his deep rolling voice. Willem did not seem aware of his own illness; his concern was all for Kik. Their handsome son had been seized the month before while helping an American parachutist reach the North Sea.

They believed Kik had been on one of the recent prison trains into Germany.

As for Father, they had learned a few more facts about his last days. He had apparently become ill in his cell and had been taken to a hospital in The Hague. There, no bed had been available. Father had died in a corridor, separated somehow from his records or any clue as to his identity. Hospital authorities had buried the unknown old man in the paupers' cemetery. The family believed they had located the particular grave.

Lieutenant Rahms stood with his back to us as we talked, staring down at the unlit stove. I opened the package that Nollie had pressed into my hand with the first embrace. It was what my leaping heart had told me: the entire Bible in a compact volume, tucked inside a small pouch with a string for wearing around the neck, as we had once carried our identity cards. I dropped it quickly over my head and down my back beneath my blouse. I could not even find words with which to thank her. The day before, in the shower line, I had given away my last remaining gospel.

"We don't know all the details," Willem was saying in a low voice to Betsie. "Just that after a few days the soldiers were taken off guard duty at the Beje and police stationed there instead." The fourth night, he believed, the chief had succeeded in assigning Rolf and another of our group to the same shift. They had found all the Jews well, though cramped and hungry, and had seen them to new hiding places.

"The time is up." Lieutenant Rahms left the stove and nodded to the notary. "Proceed with the reading of the will."

It was a brief document: The Beje was to be home for Betsie and me as long as we wanted it; should there ever be any money from the sale of house or watch shop, he knew we would recall his equal love for us all; he committed us with joy to the constant care of God.

In the silence that followed, we all bowed our heads. "Lord Jesus," Willem said, "we praise You for these moments together under the protection of this good man. How can we thank him? We have no power to do him any service. Lord, allow us to share this inheritance from our father with him as well. Take him, too, and his family into Your constant care."

12

VUGHT

"Get ready to evacuate! Collect all possessions!" The shouts of the guards echoed up and down the corridor.

I stood in the center of my cell in a frenzy of excitement. We were leaving the prison! The counter-invasion must have begun!

I grabbed the pillowcase from the cot. What riches this coarse bit of cloth had been in the two weeks since it had been provided: a shield for my head from the scratch and smell of the bedding. It almost did not matter that the promised sheets never arrived.

I dropped my few belongings into it. My Bible was in its pouch on my back. I put on my coat and hat and stood at the iron door clutching the pillowcase. An hour passed. I sat on the cot. Two hours. Three. I took off my hat and coat.

More time passed. I kept my eyes on the ant hole, hoping for a last visit from my small friends, but they did not appear. I reached into the pillowcase, took one of the crackers, and crumbled it about the little crack. No ants. They were staying safely hidden. I pressed a finger to the tiny crevice.

All at once there was a clanging out in the corridor. Doors scraped. Bolts banged. "Out! *Schnell!* No talking!"

I snatched up my hat and coat. My door screeched open. The guard was already at the next cell.

I stepped out into the hall. It was jammed from wall to wall. I had never dreamed so many women occupied this corridor. We exchanged looks.

Where would we be taken? *Not into Germany! Dear Jesus, not Germany.*

The command was given, and we shuffled forward down the long, chilly halls, each carrying a pillowcase with her belongings. At last we emerged into the wide courtyard inside the front gate of the prison, and another long wait began with the late afternoon sun on our backs. I could not see Betsie anywhere.

The huge gate swung in, and a convoy of gray transport buses drove through. I was herded aboard the third one. The seats had been removed, the windows painted over. The bus lurched as it started up, but we were standing too close together to fall. When the bus ground to a stop, we were at a freight yard somewhere on the outskirts of the city.

Again we were formed into ranks. The guards' voices were tense and shrill. We had to keep our heads facing forward, eyes front. Behind us we could hear buses arriving, then lumbering away again. Then, ahead of me, in the newest group of arriving

prisoners, I spotted Betsie! Somehow, some way, I was going to get to her!

Slowly the June day faded. At last a long row of unlit train coaches rolled slowly over the tracks in front of us. By the time the order came to board, it was pitch dark. The prisoners surged forward. Behind us the guards shouted. Obviously they were nervous at transporting so many prisoners at one time. I wriggled and shoved until at the very steps of the train, I reached out and seized Betsie's hand.

Together we climbed onto the train, together found seats in a crowded compartment, together wept in gratitude. The four months in Scheveningen had been our first separation in 53 years; it seemed to me that I could bear whatever happened with Betsie beside me.

Hours passed as the loaded train sat on the siding. Betsie told me about each of her cellmates—and I told her about mine and the little hole into which they scrambled at any emergency. As always, Betsie had given to others everything she had. The Bible that Nollie had smuggled to her she had torn up and passed around, book by book.

The train at last began to move. We pressed our faces to the glass, but no lights showed and clouds covered the moon. I must have fallen asleep, for when I opened my eyes the train had stopped. Voices were shouting at us to move. An eerie glare lit the windows. Betsie and I stumbled after the others along the aisle and down the iron steps. We seemed to have stopped in the middle of a woods. Floodlights mounted in trees lit a broad rough-cleared path lined by soldiers with leveled guns.

Spurred by the shouts of the guards, we started up the path between the gun barrels. "Keep up!" Betsie's breath was coming short and hard as they yelled at us to go faster. I took Betsie's pillowcase along with mine, hooked my other arm through hers, and hauled her along beside me.

The nightmare march lasted a mile or more. At last we came to a barbed-wire fence surrounding a row of wooden barracks. There were no beds in the one we entered, only long tables with backless benches pulled up to them. Betsie and I collapsed onto one of these. Under my arm I could feel the irregular flutter of her heart. We fell into an exhausted sleep, our heads on the table.

The sun streamed through the barracks windows when we woke up. We were thirsty and hungry—we had had nothing to eat or drink since the early meal at Scheveningen the morning before. But all that day no guard or any official person appeared

inside the barracks. At last, when the sun was low in the sky, a prisoner crew arrived with a great vat of some thick steamy substance that we gobbled ravenously.

The camp, we learned, was named Vught. Unlike Scheveningen, which had been a regular Dutch prison, Vught had been constructed especially as a concentration camp for political prisoners. We were in a kind of quarantine compound outside. Our biggest problem was idleness, wedged together as we were around the long rows of tables with nothing to do. We were guarded by the same young women who had patrolled the corridors at Scheveningen. The young guards' only technique for maintaining discipline was to shriek obscenities.

Only one of our overseers never threatened or raised her voice. This was the tall head matron from Scheveningen. She appeared in Vught the third morning, and order seized our untidy ranks. Lines straightened and whispers ceased as those cold blue eyes swept across us. Among ourselves we nicknamed her "the General."

We had been in this outer camp at Vught almost two weeks when Betsie and I, along with a dozen others, were moved again. That day, after hours of processing in this office and that office, we found ourselves marching between twisted rolls of barbed wire. We arrived in a yard surrounded on three sides by low concrete buildings. These were barracks, almost identical with the one we had left this morning, except that this one was furnished with bunks as well as tables and benches. We were not allowed to sit. There was a last wait while the matron with maddening deliberateness checked off our documents against a list.

"Betsie!" I wailed. "How long will it take?"

"Perhaps a long, long time. But what better way could there be to spend our lives?"

I turned to stare at her. "Whatever are you talking about?"

"Corrie, if people can be taught to hate, they can be taught to love! We must find the way, you and I, no matter how long it takes. . . ."

She went on, almost forgetting in her excitement to keep her voice to a whisper, while I slowly took in the fact that she was talking about our guards. I glanced at the matron seated at the desk ahead of us. I saw a gray uniform and a visored hat; Betsie saw a wounded human being.

And I wondered again what sort of a person she was, this sister of mine . . . what kind of road she followed while I trudged beside her on the all-too-solid earth.

A few days later Betsie and I were called up for work assignments. One glance at Betsie's pallid face and fragile form, and the matron waved her back inside the barracks where the elderly and infirm spent the day sewing prison uniforms. The women's uniform here in Vught was a blue overall, practical and comfortable, and a welcome change from our own clothes that we had worn since the day of our arrest.

I was told to report to the factory, actually just another large barracks inside the camp complex. I followed my escort into the single large room, where several hundred men and women sat at long plank tables covered with thousands of tiny radio parts. Two officers, one male, one female, strolled the aisle between the benches while the prisoners bent to their tasks.

I was assigned a seat at a bench and given the job of measuring small glass rods and arranging them in piles according to lengths. It was monotonous work. I longed to exchange at least names with my neighbors on either side, but the only sound in the room was the clink of metal parts and the squeak of the officers' boots.

"Production was up again last week," the male officer said in German to a tall slender man with a shaved head and a striped uniform. "You are to be commended for this increase. But we continue to receive complaints of defective wiring. Quality control must improve."

The shaved-headed man made an apologetic gesture. "If there were more food, *Herr Officier*," he murmured. "Since the cutback in rations, I see a difference. They grow sleepy, they have trouble concentrating. . . ." His voice reminded me a little of Willem's, the German with only a trace of Dutch accent.

"Then you must wake them up! If the soldiers on the front can fight on half-rations, then these lazy—"

At a look from the woman officer, he stopped. "I speak of course merely as an example. There is naturally no truth in the rumor that rations at the front are reduced. So! I hold you responsible!" And together the officers stalked from the building.

For a moment the prisoner-foreman watched them from the doorway. Slowly he raised his left hand, then dropped it with a slap to his side. The quiet room exploded. People left their benches and joined little knots of chattering friends all over the room. Half a dozen crowded around me: Who was I? Where was I from? Did I have any news of the war?

After perhaps half an hour of visiting among the tables, the foreman reminded us that we had a day's quota to meet. The foreman's name, I learned, was Moorman. He came over to my workbench the third day I was there; he had heard that I had followed the entire assembly line, tracing what became of my little piles of rods. "You're the first woman worker," he said, "who has shown interest in what we are making here."

"I am very interested," I said. "I'm a watchmaker."

He stared at me with new interest. "Then I have work you will enjoy more." He took me to the opposite end of the huge shed, where the final assembly of relay switches was done. It was intricate and exacting work, though not nearly so hard as watch repair, and Mr. Moorman was right. I enjoyed it, and it helped make the eleven-hour workday go faster.

Not only to me but to all the workers, Mr. Moorman acted more as a kindly older brother than a crew boss. I would watch him moving among his hundreds of charges, counseling, encouraging, finding a simpler job for the weary, a harder one for the restless. He stopped frequently at my bench in the first weeks. Eventually his eyes traveled to the row of relay switches in front of me.

"Dear watch lady! Can you not remember for whom you are working? These radios are for their fighter planes!" And reaching across me he would yank a wire from its housing or twist a tiny tube from an assembly. "Now solder them back wrong. And not so fast! You're over the day's quota and it's not yet noon."

At lunchtime prisoners on kitchen detail lugged in great buckets of gruel made of wheat and peas, tasteless but nourishing. Apparently there had been a cutback in rations recently. Still, the food was better and more plentiful than at Scheveningen, where there had been no noonday meal at all.

After eating, we were free for a blessed half hour to stroll about within the factory compound in the fresh air and the glorious sun. Most days I found a spot along the fence and stretched out on the warm ground to sleep (the days started with roll call at 5:00 a.m.). Sweet summer smells came in the breezes; sometimes I would dream that Karel and I were walking hand in hand along a country lane.

At 6:00 in the evening there was another roll call. Then we marched back to our various sleeping barracks. Betsie always stood in the doorway of ours waiting for me; each evening there was so much to tell one another.

"That Belgian boy and girl at the bench next to mine? This noon they became engaged!"

"Mrs. Heerma—whose granddaughter was taken to Germany—today she let me pray with her."

One day Betsie's news touched us directly. "A lady was transferred to the sewing detail today. When I introduced myself, she said, 'Another one!'"

"What did she mean?"

"Corrie, do you remember, the day we were arrested, a man came to the shop? You were sick and I had to wake you up."

I remembered very well the strange roving eyes, the uneasiness in the pit of my stomach.

"He worked with the Gestapo from the first day of occupation. He reported this woman's two brothers for Resistance work, and finally her and her husband, too. He came to Haarlem and teamed up with Willemse and Kapteyn. His name was Jan Vogel."

Flames of fire seemed to leap around that name in my heart. I thought of Father's final hours, alone in a hospital corridor. Of the underground work so abruptly halted. And I knew that if Jan Vogel stood in front of me now, I could kill him.

Betsie drew the little cloth bag from beneath her overalls and held it out to me, but I shook my head. Betsie kept the Bible during the day, since she had more chance to read and teach from it here than I did at the factory. In the evenings we held a quiet prayer meeting for as many as could crowd around our bunk.

"You lead the prayers tonight, Betsie. I have a headache."

More than a headache. All of me ached with the violence of my feelings about the man who had done us so much harm. That night I did not sleep, and the next day at my bench I scarcely heard the conversation around me. By the end of the week I had worked myself into such a sickness of body and spirit that Mr. Moorman stopped at my bench to ask if something were wrong.

"Wrong? Yes, something's wrong!" I was only too eager to tell Mr. Moorman and all Holland how Jan Vogel had betrayed his country.

What puzzled me was Betsie. She suffered everything I suffered, and yet she seemed to carry no rage. "Betsie!" I hissed one dark night when I knew that my restless tossing must be keeping her awake. Three of us now shared this single cot, as the crowded camp daily received new arrivals. "Betsie, don't you feel anything about Jan Vogel?"

"Oh, yes, Corrie! Terribly! I've felt for him ever since I knew—and pray for him whenever his name comes into my mind. How he must be suffering!"

For a long time I lay silent. Once again I had the feeling that this sister with whom I had spent all my life belonged somehow to another order of beings. Wasn't she telling me in her gentle way that I was as guilty as Jan Vogel? For I had murdered him with my heart and with my tongue.

"Lord Jesus," I whispered, "I forgive Jan Vogel as I pray that You will forgive me. I have done him great damage. Bless him now, and his family. . . ." That night, for the first time since our betrayer had a name, I slept deep and dreamlessly.

The days in Vught were a baffling mixture of good and bad. Morning roll call was often cruelly long as we stood at attention until our backs ached and our legs cramped. But the summer air was warm and alive with birds as the day approached. Gradually, a pink-and-gold sunrise would light the sky as Betsie and I squeezed each other's hands in awe.

At 5:30 we had black bread and bitter coffee, and then marched off to the various work details. I looked forward to this hike to the factory. Part of the way, we walked beside a small woods. We also marched past a section of the men's camp, and many of our group strained to identify a husband or a son among the shaved heads and striped overalls.

I was grateful to be again with people. But what I had not realized in solitary confinement was that to have companions meant to have their griefs, as well. We all suffered with the women whose men were in this camp. The discipline in the male section was much harsher than in the women's, and executions were frequent. Almost every day, gunshots would send the anguished whispers flying.

Yet in spite of sorrow and anxiety—and no one in that place was without both—there was laughter, too, in the factory when guards were not around. An impersonation of the blustering second lieutenant. A game of blind-man's bluff. A song passed in rounds from bench to bench.

During the long, hot afternoons, talk died down as each one sat alone with his or her own thoughts. I scratched on the side of the table the number of days until September 1. I had heard a chance remark that six months was the usual prison term for ration-card offenders. If that were the charge and if they included the time served at Scheveningen, September 1 would be our release date!

"Corrie," Betsie warned, "we don't know."

I had the feeling, almost, that to Betsie it did not matter. I looked at her, sitting on our cot in the last moments before lights out, sewing up a split seam in my overalls as she had so often sat mending under the lamplight in the dining room. Betsie, by the very way she sat, evoked a high-backed chair behind her and a carpet at her feet instead of this endless row of metal cots on a bare floor. I had the feeling she was as content to be reading the Bible here in Vught to those who had never heard it as she had been serving soup to hungry people in the hallway of the Beje.

As for me, I set my heart every day more firmly on September 1.

And then, all of a sudden, it looked as though we would not have to wait even this long. The Princess Irene Brigade was rumored to be in France, moving toward Belgium. The Brigade was part of the Dutch forces that had escaped to England; now it was marching to reclaim its own.

The guards were tense. The sound of the firing squad was heard more and more often. Rumor was all we lived on as we waited out the days. Women who had stayed away from the whispered prayer service around our cot now crowded close.

September 1 came and went.

Several days later we awoke to the sound of distant explosions. Long before the roll-call whistle, the entire barracks was up and milling about in the dark between the cots. Was it bombs? Artillery fire? Everyone's mind turned homeward, everyone talked of what she would do first.

At the factory Mr. Moorman tried to calm us. "Those aren't bombs," he said, "and certainly not guns. That's demolition work. Germans. They're probably blowing up bridges. It means they expect an attack, but it might not come for weeks."

But as the blasts came closer, nothing could keep down hope. Now they were so near they hurt our ears.

"Drop your lower jaw!" Mr. Moorman called out. "Keep your mouth open and save your eardrums."

After lunch the order came to return to dormitories. With sudden urgency, women embraced husbands and sweethearts who worked beside them at the factory.

Betsie was waiting for me outside our barracks. "Corrie! Has the Brigade come? Are we free?"

"I don't know. Oh, Betsie, why am I so frightened?"

The loudspeaker in the men's camp was sounding the signal for roll call. No order was given us, and we drifted about aimlessly, listening. Names were being read through the men's speaker, though it was too far way to make them out.

Suddenly an insane fear gripped the waiting women. The loudspeaker had fallen silent. We exchanged wordless looks.

Then rifle fire split the air. Around us women began to weep. A second volley. A third. For two hours the executions went on. Someone counted. More than seven hundred male prisoners were killed that day.

There was little sleeping in our barracks that night. In the morning we were ordered to collect our personal things. Betsie and I put our belongings into the pillowcases, including a small bottle of Davitamon oil—vitamin oil—that had come in a Red

Cross package. I transferred the Bible in its bag from Betsie's back to my own; she was so thin it made a visible bump between her shoulders.

About noon the marched exodus from camp began. Betsie hung hard to my arm; she was laboring for breath as she always did when she had to walk any distance. I slipped my arm beneath Betsie's shoulders and half-carried her. At last the path ended and we lined up facing the single railroad track, over a thousand women standing toe to heel. Farther along, the men's section was also at the siding.

Freight cars standing on the tracks were for us. Already the men were being prodded aboard, clambering up over the high sides. We could not see the engine, just this row of small, high-wheeled boxcars stretching out of sight in both directions, machine guns mounted at intervals on the roof. Soldiers approached along the track, pausing at each car to haul open the heavy sliding door. In front of us a gaping black interior appeared. Women began to press forward, and we were swept along with the others. Betsie's chest was still heaving after the rapid march. I had to boost her over the side of the train.

At first I could make out nothing in the dark car; then in a corner I saw a stack of bread, dozens of flat black loaves piled one on top of another. We were shoved against the back wall. Thirty or forty people were all that could fit in. Still the soldiers drove women over the side, jabbing with their guns. When eighty women were packed inside, the door thumped shut and we heard iron bolts driven into place.

Women sobbed and many fainted, although in the tight-wedged crowd they remained upright. It seemed certain that those in the middle would suffocate or be trampled to death, but we worked out a system where, by half-sitting, half-lying with our legs around one another like members of a sledding team, we were able to get down on the floor of the car.

"Do you know what I am thankful for?" Betsie's gentle voice startled me. "I am thankful that Father is in heaven today!"

Oh, Father, how could I have wept for you?

The warm sun beat down on the motionless train, the temperature in the packed car rose, the air grew foul. Beside me someone was tugging at a nail in the ancient wood of the wall. At last it came free; with the point, she set to work gouging the hole wider. Others around the sides took up the idea and in a while blessed whiffs of outside air began to circle about us.

It was hours before the train began to move. Almost at once it stopped again, then again crawled forward. The rest of the day and into the night it was the same, stopping, starting, slamming, jerking. Once when it was my turn at the air-hole, I saw in the moonlight trainmen carrying a length of twisted rail. Tracks ahead must be destroyed. I passed the news. Maybe they would not be able to repair them. Maybe we would still be in Holland when liberation came.

Betsie's forehead was hot to my hand. The girl behind me squeezed herself into an even tighter crouch so that Betsie could lie almost flat across my lap. I dozed, too, from time to time, my head on the shoulder of the kind girl behind us. Once I dreamed I could hear hailstones on Tante Jans' front windows. I opened my eyes. It really was hailing. I could hear it rattling against the side of the car.

Everyone was awake now. Another storm of hail. And then we heard a burst of machine-gun fire from the roof of the train.

"It's bullets!" someone shouted. "They're attacking the train."

Again we heard that sound like tiny stones striking the wall, and again the machine guns answered. The firing died away. For an hour the train sat motionless. Then slowly we crawled forward.

At dawn we crossed the border. We were in Germany.

13

RAVENSBRUCK

For two days and nights we were carried deep into the land of our fears. Occasionally the loaves of bread were passed around. But no provision had been made for sanitation, and the air in the car was such that few could eat.

More terrible than the crush of bodies and the filth, the single obsession was something to drink. Two or three times when the train stopped, the door was slid open a few inches and a pail of water passed in. But we had become animals, incapable of plan or system. Those near the door got it all.

On the morning of the fourth day, the train stopped again and the door was opened its full width. Like infants, on hands and knees, we crawled to the opening and lowered ourselves over the side. In front of us was a blue lake. On the far side, among sycamore trees, rose a white church steeple.

The stronger prisoners hauled buckets of water from the lake. We drank through cracked and swollen lips. The cars carrying the men had disappeared. Only a handful of soldiers—some of them looking no older than fifteen—were there to guard a thousand women. No more were needed. We could scarcely walk, let alone resist.

After a while they marched us off. For a mile the road followed the shore of the lake, and then left it to climb a hill. I wondered if Betsie could make it to the top, but the sight of trees and sky had revived her and she supported me as much as I her. We passed a number of local people on foot and in horse-drawn wagons. The children seemed wonderful to me, pink-cheeked and healthy. They returned my stares with wide-eyed interest; the adults, however, turned their heads away.

From the crest of the hill we saw it—a city of low gray barracks surrounded by concrete walls on which guard towers rose at intervals. In the very center, a square smokestack emitted a thin gray vapor into the sky.

"Ravensbruck!"

The word passed back through the lines. This was the notorious death camp whose name we had heard even in Haarlem. As Betsie and I stumbled down the hill, I felt the Bible bumping between my shoulder blades. God's Good News. Was it to this world that He had spoken it?

Now we were close enough to see the skull-and-crossbones on the walls to warn of electrified wiring along the top. The massive iron gates swung in; we marched between them. Acres of soot-gray barracks stretched ahead of us. Just inside the wall was a row of water spigots. We charged them, thrusting hands, arms, legs, even heads under the streams of water, washing away the stench of the boxcars. A squad of women guards rushed at us, shouting and driving us back from the faucets. We were herded down an avenue between barracks. This camp appeared far grimmer than the one we had left. It was set down in a long man-made valley rising on every side to those towering wire-topped walls.

At last we halted. In front of us a vast canvas-tent roof—no sides—covered an acre or more of straw-strewn ground. Betsie and I found a spot on the edge of this area and sank down. Instantly we were on our feet again. Lice! The straw was alive with them. We stood for a while, clutching belongings away from the infested ground. But at last we spread our blankets over the squirming straw and sat on them.

Some of the prisoners had brought scissors. Everywhere beneath the huge tent, women were cutting one another's hair to discourage the lice. Of course we must do the same; long hair was folly in such a place. But as I cut Betsie's waves, I cried.

Toward evening there was a commotion at one end of the tent. A line of S.S. guards was moving across it, driving women out from under the canvas. We scrambled to our feet and snatched up our blankets as they bore down upon us. Perhaps a hundred yards beyond the tent the chase stopped. We stood about, uncertain what to do. Whether a new group of prisoners had arrived or what the reason was for driving us from the tent, no one knew. Women began spreading their blankets on the hard cinder ground. Slowly it dawned on Betsie and me that we were to spend the night here where we stood. We laid my blanket on the ground, stretched out side by side, and pulled hers over us.

"The night is dark and I am far from home. . . ." Betsie's sweet soprano was picked up by voices all around us. "Lead Thou me on. . . ."

We were woken up sometime in the middle of the night by a clap of thunder and a deluge of rain. The blankets soaked through and water gathered in puddles beneath us. In the morning, our faces were black from the cinder mud.

We were still wringing water from our blankets when the command came to line up for coffee. There was a slice of black bread for each prisoner, then nothing more until we were given a ladle of turnip soup and a small boiled potato late in the afternoon.

In between we were kept standing at rigid attention on the soggy ground where we had spent the night. We were near one edge of the huge camp, close enough to the outer wall to see the triple row of electric wires running along the top. Two entire days we spent this way, stretching out again the second night right where we stood. It did not rain again, but ground and blankets were still damp. Betsie began to cough. I took Nollie's blue sweater from my pillowcase, wrapped it around her, and gave her a few drops of the vitamin oil. By morning she had agonizing intestinal cramps.

On the third night the order came to report to the processing center. A ten-minute march brought us to the building. We inched along a corridor into a huge reception room. There under the harsh ceiling lights we saw a dismal sight. As each woman reached a desk where some officers sat, she had to lay whatever she carried onto a growing pile. A few desks further along she had to strip off every scrap of clothes, throw them onto a second pile, and walk naked past the scrutiny of a dozen S.S. men into the shower room. Coming out of the shower, each woman would put on only a thin prison dress and a pair of shoes.

But Betsie needed that sweater! She needed the vitamins! Most of all, we needed our Bible. How could we live in this place without it?

We were almost at the first desk. I fished in my pillowcase, drew out the bottle of vitamins, and closed my fist around them. Reluctantly we dropped the other things on the heap that was fast becoming a mountain. "Dear God," I prayed, "You have given us this precious Book, You have kept it hidden through checkpoints and inspections, You have used it for so many—"

I felt Betsie stagger against me and looked at her in alarm. Her face was white, her lips pressed tight together. I begged a guard in German to show us the toilets. He jerked his head in the direction of the shower room.

Betsie and I stepped out of line and walked to the door of the big, dank-smelling room with its row on row of overhead spigots. It was empty, waiting for the next batch of fifty naked and shivering women to be admitted.

"Please," I said to the S.S. man guarding the door, "where are the toilets?"

"Use the drain holes!" he snapped, and as we stepped inside, he slammed the door behind us. We stood alone in the room where a few minutes later we would return stripped of the clothes on our backs. Here were the prison things we were to put on, piled just inside the door. Then we saw a pile of benches stacked in the corner. They were slimy with mildew, crawling with cockroaches, but to me they seemed the furniture of heaven itself.

"Take the sweater off!" I hissed, fumbling with the string at my neck. Betsie handed it to me, and in an instant I had wrapped it around the Bible and the vitamin bottle and stuffed the bundle behind the benches.

So when we were herded into that room ten minutes later, we were not poor, but rich. Rich in this new evidence of the care of Him who was God even of Ravensbruck.

We stood beneath the spigots as long as the flow of icy water lasted, feeling it soften our lice-eaten skin. Then we clustered dripping wet around the heap of prison dresses, holding them up, looking for approximate fits. I squirmed into a dress and then reached behind the benches and shoved the little bundle quickly inside the neck.

It made a bulge you could have seen across the Grote Markt. I flattened it out as best I could, but there was no real concealing it beneath the thin cotton dress. All the while I had the incredible feeling that it did not matter, that all I had to do was walk straight ahead.

As we trooped back out through the shower room door, the S.S. men ran their hands over every prisoner, front, back, and sides. The woman ahead of me was searched three times. Behind me, Betsie was searched. No hand touched me.

At the exit door to the building was a second ordeal, a line of women guards examining each prisoner again. I slowed down, but a guard shoved me. "Move along! You're holding up the line!"

Betsie and I arrived in Barracks 8, bringing not only the Bible, but a new knowledge of the power of God. There were three women already asleep in the bed assigned to us. They made room for us as best they could, but the mattress sloped and I kept sliding to the floor. At last all five of us lay sideways across the bed and managed to get shoulders and elbows arranged. The blanket was threadbare, but the overcrowding produced its own warmth. Betsie had put on the blue sweater beneath her dress. Now that she was wedged now between me and the others, her shivering gradually subsided, and she was asleep. I lay awake a while longer, watching a searchlight sweep the wall in long regular arcs.

Life grew harder. There was too much misery, too much suffering. Every day something grew too heavy. *Will You carry this, Lord Jesus?*

But as the rest of the world grew stranger, one thing became increasingly clear. And that was the reason the two of us were here. From morning until lights-out, whenever we were not in ranks for roll call, our Bible was the center of an ever-widening circle of help and hope. We gathered around it, holding out our hearts to its warmth and light. The blacker the night around us grew, the brighter and truer burned the Word of God. "Who shall separate us from the love of Christ? Shall tribulation, or distress, or persecution, or famine, or nakedness, or peril, or sword? . . . Nay, in all these things we are more than conquerors through him that loved us."

I would look about as Betsie read, watching the light leap from face to face. More than conquerors . . . It was a fact. We experienced it—poor, hated, hungry. We are more than conquerors. Not "we shall be." We are! I had believed the Bible always, but reading it now had nothing to do with belief. It now was a description of the way things were—of hell and heaven, of how men act and how God acts. I had read a thousand times the story of Jesus' arrest—how soldiers had slapped Him, laughed at Him, flogged Him. Now such happenings had faces and voices.

Every day the sun rose a little later, the bite took longer to leave the air. I worried about Betsie and her cough. I was doling out a drop of the Davitamon each morning on her piece of black bread, but how much longer could the small bottle last? "Especially," I would tell her, "if you keep sharing it around every time someone sneezes."

The move to permanent quarters came the second week in October 1944. Betsie and I stared at the long gray front of Barracks 28. Half its windows had been broken and replaced with rags. A door in the center let us into a large room where two hundred or more women bent over knitting needles. On tables between them were piles of gray woolen socks.

Our noses told us, first, that the place was filthy. Somewhere plumbing had backed up, and the bedding was soiled and rancid. Then as our eyes adjusted to the gloom, we saw that there were no individual beds at all, but great square piers stacked three high, wedged side by side and end to end with an occasional narrow aisle slicing through.

We followed our guide single file to the center of a large block. She pointed to the second tier. To reach it we had to stand on the bottom level, haul ourselves up, and then crawl across three other straw-covered platforms to reach the one that we would share with—how many? The deck above us was too close to let us sit up. We lay back, struggling against the nausea that swept over us from the reeking straw. We could hear other women finding their places.

Suddenly I sat up, striking my head on the cross-slats above. Something had pinched my leg.

"Fleas!" I cried. "The place is swarming with them!"

We scrambled across the platforms, heads low to avoid another bump, dropped down to the aisle, and edged our way to a patch of light.

"Betsie, how can we live in such a place?" I wailed.

"Show us how." It was said so matter of factly it took me a second to realize she was praying. The distinction between prayer and the rest of life seemed to be vanishing for Betsie.

"Corrie!" she said excitedly. "In the Bible this morning. Where was it? Read that part again!"

I glanced down the long dim aisle to make sure no guard was in sight, then drew the Bible from its pouch. "It was in First Thessalonians," I said. "Here it is: 'Comfort the frightened, help the weak, be patient with everyone. See that none of you repays evil for evil, but always seek to do good to one another and to all. . . .'"

"Go on," said Betsie.

"Oh, yes. 'To one another and to all. Rejoice always, pray constantly, give thanks in all circumstances—'"

"That's it, Corrie! That's His answer. 'Give thanks in all circumstances!' That's what we can do. We can thank God for everything about this new barracks!"

I stared at her, then around me at the foul-aired room.

"Such as?" I said.

"Such as being assigned here together."

I bit my lip. "Oh, yes, Lord Jesus!"

"Such as what you're holding in your hands."

I looked down at the Bible. "Thank You, dear Lord, that there was no inspection when we entered here! Thank You for all the women, here in this room, who will meet You in these pages."

"Yes," said Betsie. "Thank You for the very crowding here. Since we're packed so close, that many more will hear!" She looked at me expectantly.

"Oh, all right," I said. "Thank You for the jammed, crammed, packed, suffocating crowds."

"Thank You," Betsie went on, "for the fleas and for—"

This was too much. "Betsie, there's no way even God can make me grateful for a flea."

"'Give thanks in *all* circumstances,'" she quoted. "Fleas are part of this place where God has put us."

So we gave thanks for fleas.

Barracks 28 had been designed to hold four hundred women. There were now fourteen hundred quartered here, with more arriving as concentration camps in Poland, France, Belgium, Austria, and Holland were evacuated toward the center of Germany.

Nine of us shared our particular square, designed for four. Eight overflowing toilets served the entire room; to reach them we had to crawl not only over our own bedmates but over those on the other platforms between us and the closest aisle, always at the risk of adding too much weight to the already sagging slats and crashing down on the people beneath.

In Barracks 28 there was not a common language, and among exhausted, ill-fed people, quarrels erupted constantly. One raged now as the women sleeping nearest the windows slammed them shut against the cold. Loud voices demanded that they be raised again. Brawls were starting; we heard scuffling, slaps, sobs.

I felt Betsie's hands clasp mine. "Lord Jesus," she said aloud, "send Your peace into this room. There has been too little praying here. The very walls know it. But where You come, Lord, the spirit of strife cannot exist. . . ."

One by one the angry sounds let up.

"I'll make you a deal!" The voice spoke German with a Scandinavian accent. "You can sleep in here where it's warmer and I'll take your place by the window!"

"And add your lice to my own?" But there was a chuckle in the answer. "No thanks."

"I'll tell you what!" The third voice had a French accent. "We'll open them halfway. That way we'll be only half-frozen and you'll be only half-smothered."

A ripple of laughter widened around the room at this. I lay back on the straw and knew there was one more circumstance for which I could give thanks. Betsie had come to Barracks 28.

Roll call came at 4:30 a.m. here. A whistle roused us at 4:00, when the stampede began for the ration of bread and coffee in the center room. The count was made in the Lagerstrasse, the wide avenue leading to the hospital. There we joined the occupants of other barracks—some 35,000 at that time—stretching out of sight.

After roll call, work crews were called out. For weeks Betsie and I were assigned to the Siemens factory. This complex of mills and railroad terminals was a mile and a half from the camp. Several thousand of us marched beneath the charged wires into a world of trees and grass and horizons. The sun rose as we skirted the little lake.

The work at Siemens was sheer misery. Betsie and I had to push a heavy handcart to a railroad siding, where we unloaded large metal plates from a boxcar and wheeled them to a receiving gate at the factory. The grueling workday lasted eleven hours. At noontime we were given a boiled potato and some thin soup; those who worked inside the camp had no midday meal.

At day's end back at the barracks, we received our ladle of turnip soup. Then, as quickly as we could, Betsie and I made our way to the rear of the dormitory room, where we held our worship "service." Back here a small lightbulb cast a wan yellow circle on the wall, allowing us to read the Bible. An ever larger group of women gathered.

They were services like no others, these times in Barracks 28. A meeting might include a recital in Latin by a group of Roman Catholics, a whispered hymn by some Lutherans, and a soft-voiced chant by Eastern Orthodox women. The women around us packed the platforms, hanging over the edges.

Then either Betsie or I would open the Bible. Because only the Hollanders could understand the Dutch text, we would translate aloud in German. We would hear the words passed back along the aisles in French, Polish, Russian, Czech, back into Dutch. They were previews of heaven, these evenings beneath the lightbulb. I would know again that in darkness God's truth shines most clear.

No guard ever came near us. So many women now wanted to join us that we held a second service after evening roll call. On the Lagerstrasse we were under rigid surveillance. It was the same in the center room of the barracks: half a dozen guards or camp police always present. Yet in the large dormitory room there was almost no supervision at all. We did not understand it.

Another strange thing was happening. The Davitamon bottle continued to produce drops. It seemed impossible, so small a bottle, so many doses a day. Now, in addition to Betsie, a dozen others were taking it. I tried to save it for the very weakest— but these soon numbered 15, 20, 25. . . .

Still, every time I tilted the little bottle, a drop appeared at the top of the glass stopper. It just could not be! I held it up to the light, trying to see how much was left, but the dark brown glass was too thick to see through.

"There was a woman in the Bible," Betsie said, "whose oil jar was never empty." She turned to the book of Kings, the story of the poor widow of Zarephath who gave Elijah a room in her home.

Yes, wonderful things happened all through the Bible. But they happened here, too, now, this day and the next, as an awed little group watched the drops fall onto the daily rations of bread.

One day Mien, a young Dutch woman we had met in Vught, came to me in the food line. She was assigned to the hospital. "Look what I've got for you!"

We peered into the small sack she carried.

"Vitamins!" I whispered with joy. "Yeast compound!"

"Yes!" she hissed back. "There were several huge jars. I emptied each just the same amount."

Back at the bunk I took the bottle from the straw. "We'll finish the drops first," I decided. But that night, no matter how long I held it upside down, not another drop of Davitamon appeared.

On the first of November, Betsie and I were put to work leveling some rough ground just inside the camp wall. This, too, was back-breaking labor. At night spasms of pain gripped my legs.

But the biggest problem was Betsie's strength. One morning after a hard night's rain, we arrived to find the ground sodden and heavy. Betsie stumbled frequently as she walked to the low ground where we dumped the loads.

A guard screamed at her. "Can't you go faster?" Then the guard threw herself into a parody of Betsie's faltering walk.

The other guards and even some of the prisoners laughed. I felt a murderous anger rise. The guard was young and well fed—was it Betsie's fault that she was old and starving? But to my astonishment, Betsie laughed, too.

"That's me, all right," she admitted. "But you'd better let me totter along, or I'll have to stop altogether."

The guard's cheeks went crimson. "I'll decide who's to stop!" Snatching the leather crop from her belt, she slashed Betsie across the cheek and neck.

Without knowing I was doing it, I seized my shovel and rushed at her.

Betsie stepped in front of me before anyone had seen. "Corrie!" she pleaded. She tugged the shovel from my hand and dug it into the mud. A red stain appeared on Betsie's collar; a welt began to swell on her neck.

Betsie laid a thin hand over the whip mark. "Don't look at it, Corrie. Look at Jesus only." She drew away her hand. It was sticky with blood.

In mid-November the rains started in earnest—chilly, drenching day-long downpours. The Lagerstrasse was never dry now; even when the rain let up, deep puddles stood in the road. We often stood at attention in water up to our ankles.

Betsie's cough began to bring up blood. We went to sick call at the hospital, but the thermometer registered 102 degrees, not enough to admit her. We had to go back, again and again as Betsie's condition grew worse. To her this was simply another setting in which to talk about Jesus. Wherever she was, Betsie spoke to those around her about His nearness and His yearning to come into their lives. As her body grew weaker, her faith seemed to grow bolder. And sick call was "such an important place, Corrie! Some of these people are at the very threshold of heaven!"

One night Betsie's fever registered over the required 104 degrees. After a long wait, a nurse appeared to lead her to a hospital bed. I stayed with them as far as the door to the ward, then made my way back to the barracks.

Women crowded around me, asking after Betsie. How was she? How long would she have to stay? Lights-out blew, and the scramble into the bunks began. I hoisted myself to the middle tier and crawled across those already in place. What a difference since Betsie had come to this room! Where before this had been the moment for fighting, tonight the huge dormitory buzzed with "Sorry!" and "Excuse me!"

I found our section in the dark and squeezed into a spot in the middle. How was it possible, packed so close, to be so utterly and miserably alone?

14

THE BLUE SWEATER

In the morning a cold wet mist hung over the Lagerstrasse. I was grateful that Betsie did not have to stand outside. But the next day, my loneliness for Betsie became too much to bear. As soon as roll call was dismissed, I did a desperate thing. Mien had told me a way to get to the hospital without passing the guardpost. The latrine at the rear, she said, had a large window too warped to close tight. Since no visiting was permitted in the hospital, relatives of patients often took this way of getting inside.

In the dense fog, it was easy to get to the window unseen. I hoisted myself through it, then clapped my hand to my nose against the odor. A row of toilets stretched along one wall in a pool of their overflow. I dashed for the door, then stopped, my flesh crawling. Against this opposite wall a dozen corpses lay side by side. Some of the eyes were open and seemed to stare at the ceiling. I ducked into the hall and stood a moment, stomach knotting with the sight I had seen. After a while I started walking.

The hospital was a maze of halls and doors. Then a corridor looked familiar. At last, the ward where I had left Betsie! I walked eagerly down the aisles of cots looking from face to face.

Betsie was sitting up in a cot near the window. She looked stronger, a touch of color in her cheeks. The chance to lie still and stay indoors had already made a difference. She returned to Barracks 28 three days later, having not had any examination or medicine. Her forehead felt feverish to my touch. But the joy of having her back outweighed my anxiety. Fortunately, as a result of her hospitalization, she was given a permanent assignment to the "knitting brigade."

Those working in the sleeping rooms received little supervision, and Betsie found herself with most of the day in which to minister to those around her. She was a lightning knitter who completed her quota of socks long before noon. She kept our Bible with her and spent hours each day reading aloud from it, moving from platform to platform.

One evening when I got back to the barracks, Betsie was waiting for me, eyes twinkling "You know we've never understood why we had so much freedom in the big room," she said. "I've found out."

That afternoon, she said, there had been confusion in her knitting group about sock sizes, so they asked the supervisor to come and settle it.

"But she wouldn't. She wouldn't step through the door and neither would the guards. And you know why?" Betsie could not keep the triumph from her voice: "Because of the fleas!"

My mind rushed back to our first hour in this place. I remembered Betsie's thanks to God for creatures I could see no use for.

Several days later my work crew was ordered to the hospital for medical inspection. Once again we were to disrobe. I dropped my dress into the growing pile and joined the file of naked women. "What is this for?" I whispered to the woman ahead of me.

"Transport inspection," she hissed back.

Transport! But they must not send me away!

I passed one station after another—heart, lungs, scalp, throat—and still I was in the line, deemed healthy. I halted before a woman in a soiled white coat. She turned me around to face a chart on the wall. "Read the lowest line you can."

"I can't seem to read any of them." *Lord forgive me!* "Just the top letter. That *E*." The top letter was *F*.

The woman looked at me. "Do you want to be rejected?"

"Oh, doctor, my sister's here! She's not well! I can't leave her!"

The doctor scrawled something on a piece of paper. "Come back tomorrow to be fitted for glasses."

I read the paper. Prisoner 66730 was instructed to report for an optical fitting at 6:30 the following morning. The same time the transport convoys were loaded.

So as the huge vans rumbled down the Lagerstrasse the next day, I was waiting my turn at the eye clinic. The young man in charge was perhaps a qualified doctor, but his entire equipment consisted of a box of framed glasses. I found none that fitted and was ordered back to my work detail.

But I had no work assignment, having been marked down for transport. I walked uncertainly toward Barracks 28. I stepped into the center room. The supervisor looked up over the heads of the knitting crew.

"Number?" she said.

I gave it and she wrote it in a book. "Pick up your yarn and a pattern sheet," she went on. "You'll have to find a place on one of the beds; there's no room here."

I stood blinking in the center of the room. Then grabbing a skein of the gray wool, I dashed through the dormitory door.

So began the closest, most joyous weeks of all the time in Ravensbruck. In the sanctuary of God's fleas, Betsie and I ministered the Word of God to all in the room. We sat by deathbeds that became doorways of heaven. We watched women who had lost everything grow rich in hope. The knitters of Barracks 28 became the praying heart of the diseased body that was Ravensbruck, interceding for all in the camp—guards, under Betsie's prodding, as well as prisoners. We prayed beyond the walls for the healing of Germany, of Europe, of the world. As we prayed, God spoke to us.

Betsie was always very clear about what we were to do after the war. We were to have a large house to which people who had been damaged by concentration-camp life would come until they felt ready to live again in the normal world.

"It's such a beautiful house, Corrie! The floors are all inlaid wood, with statues set in the walls and a broad staircase sweeping down. And gardens all around it where they can plant flowers. It will do them good, Corrie, to care for flowers!"

I would stare at Betsie as she talked. She spoke as though she were describing things that she saw—as if that wide, winding staircase and those bright gardens were the reality and this cramped, filthy barracks the dream.

All the while, it grew colder. Each roll call the wind seemed sharper. The cold affected Betsie's legs. Sometimes in the morning she could not move them at all, and two of us would have to carry her between us. It was not hard—she weighed no more than a child. When we returned to the dormitory, I would rub her feet and hands.

But the week before Christmas, Betsie woke up unable to move either legs or arms. Another prisoner helped me carry Betsie outside and get permission to take her to the hospital. We carried her to the hospital, then stopped. The sick-call line stretched out of sight around the corner of the building. In the sooty snow alongside, three bodies lay where they had fallen.

We turned and carried Betsie back to the Lagerstrasse. After roll call we got her back into bed. Her speech was slow, but she was trying to say something.

"A concentration camp, Corrie. But we're . . . in charge. . . ." I had to bend very close to hear. The camp was in Germany. It was no longer a prison, but a home where people who had been warped by this philosophy of hate and force could come to learn another way. There were no walls, no barbed wire, and the barracks had windowboxes. "It will be so good for them . . . watching things grow. People can learn to love. . . ."

I knew by now which people she meant. The German people.

I looked into Betsie's face. "We are to have this camp in Germany instead, Betsie? Instead of the big house in Holland?"

"Oh, no! We have the house first! It's ready and waiting for us . . . such tall, tall windows! The sun is streaming in—"

A coughing fit seized her; when finally she lay still, a stain of blood blackened the straw. She dozed fitfully during the day and night that followed, waking several times with the excitement of some new detail about our work in Holland or Germany.

"The barracks are gray, Corrie, but we'll paint them green! Bright, light green, like springtime."

"We'll be together, Betsie? You're sure about that?"

"Always together, Corrie! You and I . . . always together."

When the siren blew next morning, we carried Betsie from the dormitory, but the guard standing at the street door stopped us. "Take her back to the bunks."

Wonderingly, we replaced Betsie on the bed. Was it possible that the atmosphere of Barracks 28 had affected even this ordinarily cruel guard? As soon as roll call was dismissed, I ran back to the dormitory. There, beside our bed, stood the guard and two orderlies from the hospital with a stretcher. The guard straightened as I approached. "Prisoner is ready for transfer," she snapped.

I looked at the woman more closely. Had she risked fleas and lice to spare Betsie the sick-call line? She did not stop me as I started after the stretcher.

Sleet stung us as we reached the outside. We walked past the waiting line of sick people, through the door, and into a large ward. They placed the stretcher on the floor and I leaned down to make out Betsie's words, ". . . must tell people that there is no pit so deep that He is not deeper still. They will listen to us, Corrie, because we have been here."

I stared at her wasted form. "When will all this happen, Betsie!"

"Very soon! By the first of the year, Corrie, we will be out of prison!"

I watched as they placed Betsie on a narrow cot close to the window. She and I exchanged smiles and soundless words, and then I was ordered back to work.

About noontime I put down my knitting and received permission to visit the hospital. I reached the door of the ward, but the nurse would not let me enter. I went around to the window next to Betsie's cot. I waited until the nurse left the room, then tapped gently.

Betsie's eyes opened. Slowly she turned her head.

"Are you all right?" I formed with my lips.

She nodded. She moved her lips in reply. ". . . so much work to do . . ."

I was not again granted permission to go to the hospital that day, but the following morning, I headed for the hospital, permission or no.

I reached the window and cupped my eyes to peer in. A nurse was standing directly between me and Betsie. I ducked out of sight, waited a minute, then looked again. A second nurse had joined the first, both now standing where I wanted to see. Then they stepped to the head and foot of the bed. I gazed curiously at what lay on it. It looked like a carving in old ivory.

It was Betsie.

The nurses had each seized two corners of the sheet. They lifted it between them and carried the bundle from the room. Where were they taking her? I began running along the side of the building, chest hurting me as I breathed.

Then I remembered the washroom. My feet carried me around to the back of the building. There, with my hand on the windowsill, I stopped. Suppose they had laid Betsie on that floor?

I started walking again, for a long time, with that pain in my chest. Each time my feet took me back to the washroom window. I would not go in. Betsie could not be there.

"Corrie!"

I turned to see Mien running after me. "I've looked for you everywhere! Oh, Corrie, come!"

She seized my arm and drew me toward the back of the hospital.

I wrenched my arm free. "I know, Mien."

She seized me again, led me to the washroom window, and pushed me in ahead of her. I turned my head to the side in that reeking room—I would not look at the bodies that lined the far wall. Mien put an arm around my shoulder and drew me across the room till we were standing above that heartbreaking row.

"Corrie! Do you see her?"

I raised my eyes to Betsie's face.

There she lay, her eyes closed as if in sleep, her face full and young. The deep hollows of hunger and disease were simply gone. In front of me was the Betsie of Haarlem, happy and at peace. Strong! Free! This was the Betsie of heaven, bursting with joy and health.

I turned wonderingly to Mien, then looked once more at the radiant face of my sister. Eventually Mien and I left the room together. A pile of clothes was heaped in the hallway; on top lay Nollie's blue sweater. But I left it behind. Now what tied me to Betsie was the hope of heaven.

The beauty of Betsie's face sustained me as I went from one to another of the women who had loved her, describing to them her peace and her joy.

15

THE THREE VISIONS

It was three mornings later when over the loudspeaker during roll call came "Ten Boom, Cornelia!"

I walked forward. Why had I been singled out?

The guard signaled me to follow her. I splashed through the slush, trying to keep up. My legs and feet were painfully swollen from the long count the day before.

I hobbled behind the guard into the administration barracks. Several prisoners were standing in line at a large desk. An officer seated behind it stamped a paper and handed it to the woman in front of him.

"*Entlassen!*" he said.

Entlassen? Released? Was the woman free?

Another prisoner stepped to the desk. A signature, a stamp: "*Entlassen!*"

At last "Ten Boom, Cornelia," was called. I stepped to the desk, steadying myself against it. He wrote, brought down the stamp, and then I was holding it in my hand: a piece of paper with my name and birth date on it, and across the top in large black letters, Certificate of Discharge.

Dazed, I followed the others through a door at our left. There at another desk I was handed a railway pass entitling me to transportation through Germany to the Dutch border. Outside this office a guard pointed me down a corridor into another room for a release physical. The prisoners who had been ahead of me were tugging their dresses over their heads and lining up against the rear wall.

I drew the Bible over my head along with the dress, rolled them together and buried the bundle at the bottom of the clothing pile. I joined the others.

When the doctor examined me, his eyes traveled down to my swollen feet.

"Edema," he said. "Hospital."

I scrambled back into my clothes and followed the trustee from the building. We started up the Lagerstrasse.

"Then I'm not to be released?"

"You will be, as soon as the swelling in your legs goes down," the trustee said. "They only release you if you're in good condition."

We walked into the hospital and into a ward at the rear. I was assigned a bed near a wall where I could keep my swollen legs elevated. That was what mattered now: to get the swelling down, to pass the inspection.

I went each morning to the clinic. Each time the verdict was "Edema of the feet and ankles." Many of those who attended the clinic were, like myself, discharged prisoners. Some had been released months ago. What if Betsie were still alive? Our prison term would have been up together. But Betsie would never have passed the physical. What if I were to pass the inspection and she . . .

There are no "ifs" in God's kingdom. I could hear her soft voice saying it. *His timing is perfect.*

In these final days, I looked for someone to give the Bible to. Not many in the ward would be able to read the Dutch text, but at last I slipped it around the neck of a grateful young woman from Holland.

Finally the doctor at the clinic stamped the medical approval on my discharge form. Events now moved with bewildering speed. I was outfitted with clothes: underthings, a woolen skirt, a silk blouse, sturdy shoes, a hat, an overcoat. I was handed a form to sign stating that I had never been ill at Ravensbruck, and that the treatment had been good. I signed.

I was given back my watch and Mama's ring, and then I waited with a group of ten or twelve just inside the gate.

The heavy iron doors swung open; we marched through. We climbed the little hill. Now I could see the lake, frozen from shore to shore. The pines sparkled in the winter sun like a Christ-mas card. At the small train station the guard left us without a backward glance. We would all be traveling as far as Berlin, and then each would pursue her separate route home The train trip itself became a blur. We reached the huge, bomb-gutted terminal in Berlin sometime after midnight. It was New Year's Day, 1945. Betsie had been right: She and I were out of prison.

The trip seemed endless. Many miles of track could be traveled only at a crawl. There were long detours. Often we did not stop in a station at all, for fear of air raids. All the while, out my window passed once-beautiful Germany—fire-blackened woods and ruined villages.

We finally crossed into Holland. Flat, snow-covered fields glided past the window. It was still occupied Holland; German soldiers still stood along the tracks—but it was home.

The train stopped at Groningen, a Dutch city near the border. Beyond that, rails were torn up. With the last of my strength, I limped to a hospital near the station.

A nurse in a sparkling white uniform invited me into her office. When I told my story, she left the room. In a few minutes she was back with a tray of tea and toast. "I left the butter off," she said. "You're suffering from malnutrition. You must be careful what you eat."

Tears tumbled into the hot tea as I drank. There were no available beds in the hospital, she said, but one of the staff was away and I was to have her room. "Right now I have a hot tub running."

I followed her down gleaming corridors in a kind of happy dream. In a large bathroom, clouds of steam rose from a glistening white tub. Nothing in my life ever felt as good as that bath. I lay submerged to my chin, feeling the warm water soothe my skin. "Just five minutes more!" I would beg each time the nurse rapped at the door.

At last I let her hand me a nightgown and lead me to a room where a bed was turned down and waiting. Sheets, top and bottom. I could not get enough of running my hands over them. The nurse tucked a second pillow beneath my swollen feet. I struggled to stay awake. To lie here clean and cared for was such joy, I did not want to sleep through a minute of it.

I stayed in the hospital at Groningen ten days, feeling my strength return. The ache in my heart was to get to Willem and Nollie. At last the hospital switchboard reached the telephone operator in Hilversum with the news of Betsie's death and my release.

Hospital authorities arranged a ride for me on an overnight food truck headed south. In the early morning the truck pulled up to Willem's big brick nursing home, and soon my arms were around Tine and two of my nieces. Willem limped down the corridor with the help of a cane. We held each other a long time while I told them the details of Betsie's illness and death.

"Almost," said Willem slowly, "I wish to have this same news of Kik. It would be good for him to be with Betsie and Father." They had had no word of this tall blond son since his deportation to Germany. I remembered his hand on my shoulder, guiding me on our bicycles through the blacked-out streets to Pickwick's. Kik! Are the young and brave as vulnerable as the old and slow?

I spent two weeks in Hilversum. But something in me could not rest until I got back to Haarlem. Nollie was there, of course. But it was the Beje, too, the house itself that called me home.

The problem was getting there. Finally, after many relayed phone calls, Willem told me the trip had been arranged. The roads were deserted as we set out to the rendezvous spot with the car from Haarlem. Pulled off onto the snow at the side of the road, we saw a long black limousine with official government plates and curtained windows. I kissed Willem good-bye and then stepped quickly, as instructed, into the rear of the limousine.

The ungainly bulk beside me was unmistakable.

"Oom Herman!" I cried.

"My dear Cornelia." His great hand closed around mine. "God permits me to see you again."

I had last seen Pickwick sitting between two soldiers on the prison bus, his bald head bruised and bleeding. Now here he was. He seemed as well informed as ever about everything that went on in Haarlem, and as the uniformed driver sped us along the empty roads, he filled me in on all the details I ached to know. Our Jews were safe except for Mary Itallie, who had been sent to Poland following an arrest in the street. There was no further word on her. Our group was still operating, although many of the young men were in hiding.

He warned me to expect changes at the Beje. After the police guard had been removed, a series of homeless families had been housed there, although at the moment the living quarters above the shop were empty. Loyal Toos had returned and reopened the watch business. The optician next door had given her space in his shop from which she took orders to give to our repairmen in their homes.

Now the limousine was threading the narrow streets of Haarlem into the Barteljorisstraat. I was out of the car almost before it stopped, running to the side door and into Nollie's embrace. She and her girls had been there all morning, sweeping, washing windows, airing sheets for my homecoming. I saw Toos, laughing because I was home and at the same time crying because Father and Betsie, the only two people she had ever allowed herself to love, would not be returning.

Together we trooped through the house and shop, looking, stroking, remembering. I stood on the landing outside the dining room and ran my hand over the smooth wood of the

Frisian clock. I could see Father stopping here: "*We mustn't let the clock run down. . . .*"

I opened the glass, moved the hands to agree with my wristwatch, and slowly drew up the weights. I was home.

And yet my restlessness continued. I was home and I soon was working, but often I would come to with a start at my workbench to realize that I had been staring into space. The repairmen Toos found—trained under Father—were excellent, so I spent less time in the shop.

I knew what it was I was looking for. It was Betsie.

I had missed her every moment since she had left Ravensbruck forever. It was Betsie I had thought to find back here in Haarlem, in the home she loved. But she was not here. Now for the first time since her death, I remembered. "We must tell people, Corrie. We must tell them what we learned. . . ."

That very week I began to speak. Through the streets and suburbs of Haarlem, I bumped on my bicycle rims, bringing the message that joy runs deeper than despair. It was news that people needed to hear that cheerless spring of 1945 when no tulips turned fields into carpets of color—the bulbs had all been eaten. No family was without its tragedy. In churches and clubs and private homes in those desperate days, I told the truths Betsie and I had learned in Ravensbruck.

At these meetings I spoke of Betsie's first vision: a home here in Holland where those who had been hurt could learn to live again unafraid. At the close of one of these talks, an elegant lady came to me. I knew her by sight: Mrs. Bierens de Haan, whose home in the suburb of Bloemendaal was said to be one of the most beautiful in Holland, though I had never seen it myself.

"I am a widow," Mrs. Bierens de Haan was saying, "but I have five sons in the Resistance. Four are alive and well. The fifth we have not heard from since he was taken to Germany. As you spoke just now, something in me said, 'Jan will come back, and in gratitude you will open your home for this vision of Betsie ten Boom.'"

Two weeks later a small boy delivered a scented envelope to the side door; inside in slanted purple letters was a single line, "Jan is home."

Mrs. Bierens de Haan herself met me at the entrance to her estate. Together we walked up an avenue of ancient oaks meeting above our heads. Rounding the final bend, I saw it, a fifty-six room mansion in the center of a vast lawn. Two gardeners were poking about the flowerbeds.

"We've let the gardens go," Mrs. Bierens de Haan said. "But I thought we might put them back in shape. Don't you think released prisoners might find therapy in growing things?"

I did not answer. I was staring up at the gabled roof and the leaded windows. Such tall, tall windows . . .

"Are there inlaid wood floors inside, and a grand gallery around a central hall, and—and statues set along the walls?"

Mrs. Bierens de Haan looked at me in surprise. "You've been here!"

"No," I said. "I heard about it from—"

How could I explain what I did not understand?

"From someone who's been here," she finished.

"Yes," I said. "From someone who's been here."

The second week in May the Allies retook Holland. The Dutch flag hung from every window, and the "Wilhelmus" was played on the liberated radio day and night. The Canadian army rushed food to the cities.

In June the first people arrived at the beautiful home in Bloemendaal. Silent or endlessly relating their losses, withdrawn or fiercely aggressive, every one was a damaged human being. Not all had been in concentration camps; some had spent two, three, even four years hidden in attic rooms and back closets here in Holland. In Bloemendaal they were reminded that they were not the only ones who had suffered. For all these people, the key to healing turned out to be the same. Each had a hurt he had to forgive: the neighbor who had reported him, the brutal guard, the sadistic soldier.

Strangely enough, it was not the Germans people had most trouble forgiving; it was their fellow Dutchmen who had sided with the enemy. These former NSB collaborators were now in pitiful condition, turned out of homes and apartments, unable to find jobs, hooted at in the streets.

I felt we should invite them to Bloemendaal, to live side by side with those they had injured, to seek a new compassion on both sides. But it was too soon for people working their way back from such hurt. The two times I tried it, it ended in open fights. So I turned the Beje over to these former NSBers.

This was how it went, those years after the war, experimenting, making mistakes, learning. The doctors, psychiatrists, and nutritionists who came free of charge to any place caring for war victims expressed surprise at our loose-run ways. At morning and evening worship, people drifted in and out, table manners were atrocious, and one man took a walk into Haarlem every morning at 3:00 a.m. I could not bring myself to sound a whistle or to scold, or to consider gates or curfews.

But in their own time, people worked out their deep pain. It often started, as Betsie had known it would, in the garden. As flowers bloomed or vegetables ripened, talk was less of the bitter past, more of tomorrow's weather. As their horizons broadened, I would tell them about the people living in the Beje, people who never had a visitor, never a piece of mail. When mention of the NSBers no longer brought on a volley of wrath, I knew the person's healing was not far away. The day he said, "Those people you spoke of—I wonder if they'd care for some homegrown carrots," I knew a miracle had taken place.

As I continued to speak, I traveled all over Holland, to other parts of Europe, to the United States. But the place where the hunger was greatest was Germany. Germany was a land in ruin, cities of ashes and rubble, but more terrifying still, minds and hearts of ashes. A great weight hung over that land.

It was at a church service in Munich that I saw him, the former S.S. man who had stood guard at the shower room door in the processing center at Ravensbruck. He was the first of our actual jailers that I had seen since that time. Suddenly it was all there—the roomful of mocking guards, the heaps of clothing, Betsie's pain-blanched face.

He came up to me as the church was emptying, beaming. "How grateful I am for your message, *Fraulein*." he said. "To think that, as you say, He has washed my sins away!"

His hand was thrust out to shake mine. And I, who had preached so often to the people in Bloemendaal the need to forgive, kept my hand at my side. Even as the angry, vengeful thoughts boiled through me, I saw the sin of them. *Lord Jesus,* I prayed, *forgive me and help me to forgive him.*

I struggled to raise my hand. I could not. Again I breathed a silent prayer. *Jesus, I cannot forgive him. Give Your forgiveness.*

As I took his hand the most incredible thing happened. From my shoulder along my arm and through my hand, a current seemed to pass from me to him, while into my heart sprang a love for this stranger that almost overwhelmed me.

I discovered that it is not on our forgiveness any more than on our goodness that the world's healing hinges, but on His. When He tells us to love our enemies, He gives, along with the command, the love itself.

Many months later, a director of a relief organization came to see me. They had heard of my rehabilitation work in Holland. "We've located a place for the work," he said. "A former concentration camp."

We drove to Darmstadt to look over the camp. Rolls of rusting barbed wire still surrounded it. I walked up a cinder path between drab gray barracks.

"Windowboxes," I said. "We'll have them at every window. The barbed wire must come down, of course, and then we'll need paint. Bright green, the color of things coming up new in the spring. . . ."

SINCE THEN

Working with a committee of the German Lutheran Church, Corrie opened the camp in Darmstadt as a home and place of renewal. It functioned in this way until 1960, when it was torn down to make room for new construction in a thriving new Germany.

The home in Bloemendaal served war victims until 1950, when it also began to receive people in need of care from the population at large. It is still in operation today, in its own new building, with patients from many parts of Europe.

Willem died in December 1946. Just before his death, he opened his eyes to tell Tine, "It is well with Kik." It was not until 1953 that the family learned definitely that Kik had died in 1944 at the concentration camp in Bergen-Belsen. Today a "Ten Boom Street" in Hilversum honors Kik.

Peter van Woerden dedicated his musical gifts to God's service. He eventually traveled with his wife and five children as a family singing group, bearing the message of God's love throughout Europe and the Middle East.

In 1959 Corrie was part of a group that visited Ravensbruck to honor Betsie and the 96,000 other women who died there. There Corrie learned that her own release had been part of a clerical error; one week later all women her age were killed.

When I heard Corrie speak in Darmstadt in 1968, she was 76, still traveling ceaselessly. Her work took her to 61 countries, sharing the truth the sisters learned in Ravensbruck: Jesus can turn loss into glory.

John and I made some of those trips with her, the only way to catch this busy woman long enough to get the information we needed to tell her story. Our best talks came during the times she stayed in our home. Our kids loved her visits, loved her ability to laugh at herself—like the time the chocolate ice cream from the first cone she had ever eaten kept running down her hand onto her blouse and shoes. "No, Aunt Corrie! You have to lick around the bottom of the scoop. Watch—like this!" Most of all, they loved the fact that each of them was as important to her as the loftiest church leader or city mayor.

In her mid-eighties, failing health brought an end to Corrie's missionary journeys. Friends provided Corrie a house in California, but even bedridden, Corrie never stopped witnessing to God's love. If you would come to cheer her up, you would be the one who would leave that bedroom, spirit mysteriously and gloriously renewed.

At 11:00 at night on her 91st birthday—April 15, 1983—Corrie, in the phrase she had always used, "went home" at last.

Elizabeth Sherrill

Elizabeth and John Sherrill met as young people on board the *Queen Elizabeth* and were later married in Switzerland. Together they have published several thousand articles and written more than thirty books, including *The Cross and the Switchblade* with David Wilkerson and *God's Smuggler* with Brother Andrew. The Sherrills' writing has taken them to five continents, and their work still keeps them on the road, reporting the Holy Spirit's awe-inspiring deeds in the 21st century.